THE PHILOSOPHY OF CONAN THE BARBARIAN

And the theory of human sexuality as the cause of barbarian invasions

Bozidar Maslac

To my father

TABLE OF CONTENTS

INTRODUCTION

What did I want to accomplish with this book? To explain this, I have to mention an event that changed the direction of my life. A paranormal experience that happened to me in 2000 has influenced my whole personality. I wouldn't go into the details of that event, so I'll only emphasize some main points. At the time of the last year of the Second Millennium and Serbia's October Revolution, a super intelligent being tried to reach me. It tried to help me to realize certain truths by myself in an associative way. I have to mention that I was a very curious child from a young age and that I was one of those children who enjoyed reading the most diverse literature. Introvert and turned to a book till my twenties, I've read a whole bunch of literature, out of pure curiosity. The mentioned being seemed to have tried to help me extract some system from the accumulated data I had. The catalyst for the whole process was a girl, who I met at the time and for me she was a true fatal woman.

At the beginning of that process, I fell into a state of contemplation, i.e. the process of knowing a system of necessary truths that made me feel blissful and happy. At one point, that process got its dark side. Another being, ancient, powerful and evil, tried to incarnate[1i] in my spirit. I had the feeling of being someone else, someone who had a task to do something important and evil in this world. By a lucky twist of fate, or God's help, I managed to regain my personality, but I lost my peace. Some demon was still existing inside me. Driven by that inarticulate urge, I enrolled in philosophy studies in 2003, and the knowledge I gained from studies helped me in writing this book. When I wrote this book, I

---

[1] Similar to the case of Charles Dexter Ward described in Lovecraft's book with the same title – *The Case of Charles Dexter Ward*.

regained some of my inner peace. As if I was going through a spiritual pregnancy for a decade, a state of elevated spiritual libido, which disappeared with the completion of this book. Who knows, maybe the demon in me found the new place of existence in my book? Maybe in my writing, there's a hidden message that isn't the work of my conscious personality, but something hidden in the deep ocean of the unconscious? A message that someone will interpret in the right way one day.

Why did I take *Conan the Barbarian* as the theme of my first book? At an acute moment of my transformation, I had an obsessive urge to rent that movie at a video store, which I did. The movie has served me in the way the other illiterate clairvoyants used books to focus on certain visions. Later, in my usual state of mind, I've watched the film for several times, revealing in it all the beauty of Milius's portrayal of some eternal philosophical problems and truths. I've realized that this masterpiece is filled with philosophical ideas, probably more than any other movie made so far. The book contains reflections on the movie itself, occasionally extending to the issues that are presented or only touched upon in *Conan the Barbarian*. In some chapters, I sometimes only mention the movie, primarily dealing with philosophical problems. In the second part of the book, I present my synthesis of Kant's aspiration for universality and formality with Nietzsche's immoral dualism. I believe that I've made an original contribution to ethics with my approach, which solves Kant's problematic, counter-intuitive example from his essay *On a supposed right to lie from philanthropy* and many other problems of universalism. Using the knowledge of evolution and sexuality, I've come up with a solution to a historical problem related to the collapse of urban/civic civilization. Why are civilizations destroyed or conquered by barbarians? I've presented the complex processes underlying those historical events in a very simple and logically consistent way that takes the form of regularity, which allows history and sociology to become much more serious sciences. It's important to emphasize that I use and interpret the epic, poetic heritage of my people in my own way, according to the tradition of the culture, where I come from. In doing so, I don't differ from the Greek philosophers. I think we should pay attention to the interpretation of the epic poetry that I present in this book. I've used that poetic heritage in the analysis of three major problems: film-artistic, ethical, and historical-sociological.

From the above mentioned, it's clear that my book is a triptych. It consists of three aspects that are linked with the theme of barbarians and the masterpiece *Conan the Barbarian.* I'm sure it's interesting to read, and that curious people will be glad to read something like this. I also count on fans of the opus about *Conan the Barbarian,* whose number isn't small. The iconography of that movie has found a place in domestic culture as well. It appears in a few movies. In the movie *Decko koji obecava*[2], the party is organized in a space with the photo of Conan the Barbarian with an interesting symbolism.

I have to end with the following. One might say that this is the work of a person to whom Jung's "Inflation with the Wise Old Man" happened. I'm not going to deny it. However, my opinion regarding knowledge is that it doesn't matter how we get it but what truth it reveals to us.

---

[2] A Promising Boy

PART ONE - BARBARIAN

CHILD IN IRON AGE

In order to manage the world, first we have to manage time and space. It's similar with a piece of art. In order to understand a play in a theater, it's necessary to understand that stage is something that separates us and the rest of the world from that work of art. A picture frame helps us disconnect from the rest of the world and focus on the work itself. In literary creation, if the action isn't set in the contemporary moment of writing, an artist must strive to convince us in the age, where the action is set, to separate us from the world and keep our attention. Besides such cases, there are works that are set in fictional space and time. Here, by space we mean fictional geography. Alice, by a twist of fate, gets into Wonderland, which is a fictional space. In film art, movies are often set in the fictional dimensions we've mentioned. Many science fiction movies, genre that has become dominant in film art lately, are set in fictional places and times. *Avatar*, financially the most successful movie of all time[3], takes place in such a place and time. But is imagination really that successful? Can it really create a whole new world? In the case of *Avatar*, most of it has already been seen. Aliens are humanoids, who live in a hunter-gatherer society. They have an animistic religion (similar to Earthlings, who are the same type of culture) and ride domesticated animals. They're armed with earthlike weapons at that stage of civilization (such as spears), and they, more or less, resemble the American Natives, except that they are blue skinned. A white man, who starts living with them and finds himself in that lifestyle and who then confronts his own people and race, is also

---

[3] Written in 2010

the theme already seen in Western movies. Movies like *Dancing with the Wolves* and *Pocahontas* have a story similar to that in Avatar. The very message conveyed in the movie - that it's necessary to live in harmony with nature - is similar to the lessons of hunter-gatherer cultures, which are directed to the conservation of hunting grounds and animals, which they depend on.

Our intention isn't to criticize, but to show how difficult it is to create something truly original. Much stranger and more original alien is the ocean on the planet Solaris in *Solaris* by Stanislaw Lem. That book has been adapted into a movie with the same name, made by well-known and respected Russian director Andrei Tarkovsky, director of movies such as *Andrei Rublev* and *Stalker*. Although some artists are original, that trait isn't necessary for a good artist. He can tell a well-known story in a new way, and the way something is presented is the most important for a work of art. In *Conan the Barbarian*, the way the philosophy has been portrayed has turned the whole movie into an artistic masterpiece. Nevertheless, we'll see that this movie is also original. We'll show why *Conan the Barbarian* is a powerful work of art. Let's try at the beginning of our enterprise to determine the location and time of *Conan the Barbarian*. To what extent are the space and time, where this movie is set, are fictional? Has the author used the actual period of the human past in creating that piece to make it more real?

At the beginning of the movie, Conan's chronicler dates the events he describes between the sinking of Atlantis, which, if you believe to Plato, was somewhere around 9500 BC, and the birth of Arius's sons, which is something more difficult to date. There's certainly no reference to Arius, the founder of Aryan teaching within Christianity, who was proclaimed a heretic at a church council in Nicaea in 325 and died in 336. Here Arius could be a Latinized version of the name Ari (Aria), which originates from *Ari* (Proto-Indo-European —meaning noble). Aryan people, a powerful group of Indo-European peoples that spread over the Iranian plateau and across northern India during the first half of the II millennium BC, were named as a reference to that term. One branch of Indo-European languages was named Indo-Aryan after Aryan people and it includes Farsi, Hindi, Bengali and some other living languages. Also, names Plato (Plato's true name is Aristocles) and Aristotle have roots in old Indo-European languages. *Ari* in their names means the best.

The term Aryan became popular during and after the Second World War due to its Nazi meaning. Believing that some races were born to rule over others, the term Aryan[4] was used by the Nazis to refer to the ruling race of pure white blood, blond hair and blue eyes (In fact, it was an ideal; belonging was determined by larger set of properties). Of course, according to that interpretation, the Germans were descendants of Aryans, but here and there mixed with lower races such as the Jews. That's why in the Third Reich there were racial laws that forbade marriages between Aryans and "lower races" and everything else that wasn't in line with the logic of such an ideology. Nietzsche's idea of "overman", as it isn't clearly defined by Nietzsche and it's reduced to a set of predicates, has contributed to a freer Nazi's interpretation and has a part in the interpretation of that "super" race. Nietzsche admired the caste system in India, where one knows who rules and who obeys, and he used terms such as "great blond beast" for the prehistoric prototype of "overman" (this term will be discussed later). Therefore, the Nazi interpretation of the "overman" isn't completely groundless, but it should be emphasized that Nietzsche considered the Poles better than the Germans, and he wasn't even an anti-Semite.

The above mentioned isn't irrelevant to our subject since some terms are used in everyday communication without first knowing their genesis. For our purposes, it'll be sufficient to guess

---

[4]In fact, descendants of the historical Aryans are still present in India today. They certainly aren't blond and blue-eyed, and they genetically are more similar to the Slavs than to Germans. Yet, the term has become so common that it now relates to the white race of European descent, and it's nowadays its primary meaning in slang.

that the Cimmerian's adventures happened in the period between 9500 BC and, roughly, around 2000 BC. Although at first sight knowing the year isn't that important, but it'll help us understand the period and circumstances where our hero lives. Milius has set the movie in the mythical age, which is dark and unknown, but he also uses the material from an actual historical, i.e. archeological period, which is filled with myths and mysteries too. Already in the first scene of the movie, when the molten iron mass takes the form of a sword, we notice that Milius has set his story in the Iron Age. After all, the plot also reminds of the transition period from the Bronze Age to the Iron Age. Mythical period, Conan's period, and the true - Iron Age, blend in.

The name of Conan's people is also related to that. It's common to use the term *the Cimmerians* for Conan's people. However, Robert E. Howard, the author of books *Conan the Barbarian*, didn't use so much his imagination while giving names to peoples and geographical places. He used true references, so the Picts, Khitai, Vendhya, Stix, Hyrkania etc. are names of peoples and geographical places taken from true history and ancient mythology. The Cimmerians (Kimmerians) are the people that really existed. The Cimmerians were known as the bearers of the Iron Culture and according to Herodotus they lived in the area north of the Caucasus and the Black Sea. According to Assyrian records, which chronologically precede Herodotus, the Cimmerians were located south of the Caucasus. Gamora is a town historically related to the Cimmerians, while Conan (Milius's Conan, not Howard's and in future we'll refer to Milius's Conan, and we'll stress that it refers to Howard's Conan when it comes to him) refers to Zamora, the crossroads of the worlds, to find the villains who hurt him.

In order to understand the ideas of honor and dignity of those people, we'll mention the following event. The Cimmerians were driven away by the Scythians from their territory. Before the Cimmerians left their territory, the Cimmerian nobles from the royal family had fought against each other to death to be buried in their homeland. Their bodies were buried by ordinary people, who then fled before the Scythians. The Cimmerians spread across different countries, fighting for their new territory. They killed the Lydian king Gyges, who then served as the character in the myth of the Ring of Gyges. They were also attacking Greek Ionian colonies in Asia Minor. There hasn't been much heard of them since the mid-7th century BC. They probably suffered great plague epidemic damage that hit them at the time. The Thracians could be the Cimmerians' descendants who went to Europe. The revolution in iron-making in Europe, well-known Hallstatt culture, could be linked to the influence of the Thraco-Cimmerian culture on the Celts. After all, the Conan's name itself, which is of Celtic origin and means Little Wolf, testifies to the fact that Robert E. Howard was informed or suspected of that. That name is still very popular in Celtic countries nowadays.

So far, we've been trying to show the age when Conan lived to understand how Howard and Milius used real knowledge of the past to create as convincing work of art as possible. Using the right references is a good artistic approach. Although art doesn't have to be and shouldn't be a slave to realism, it's better when we feel the real atmosphere in order to overcome the psychological wall that divides the stage (or canvas) from our involvement in the work of art itself. This is even more important when you portray a place, time, people, and values that are vastly different from the experiences of a consumer of a certain artistic achievement. Nowadays, the artistic heritage of generations has made it possible for a creator to get straight to the point, which couldn't have been implied earlier. Let's imagine you are writing a book about some fantastic beings. If you're writing about aliens you don't have to explain that the existence of aliens is logically and scientifically possible –it's implied. But, the pioneers in that field had to make an introduction, to explain to the reader what they were writing about. They needed to define the term, and the best way to do it is to use artistic means to create such a definition. In doing so, art doesn't define its terms the way a scientist or philosopher would do it. A roundabout way is the path of art; you need to feel something first, by intuition, emotion, and artistic sense. In science or mathematics, the definition should be as clear as possible, unambiguous; it mustn't leave any space for our imagination to add predicates that aren't contained in the idea of the defined. Art has the opposite goal; art wants to present us something that opposes definition. When Milius presents the smithy, where Conan's father makes swords, he can't have a systematical approach and tell us - that's bellow, it is used for this and that, and that's a mold, it must be such and such, this iron here has a certain amount of carbon that will make it harder and increase the chance of sharpening. We need to experience the smithy in a natural way, like we experience the greatest number of objects in our lives. We won't know the sword through its molecular structure, but we'll see its gray-blue color, shine, we'll feel the coldness of its blade and its sharpness that has its purpose we'll feel it by touching it, by our sense combined with intuition. We'll learn about the smithy through the heat in it, the color of molten metal, the form of incandescent coal, the resistance that metal puts up when forging. Heidegger, whose aesthetics guided us in this paragraph, stresses such a distinction between science and art.

Nietzsche, on the other hand, whose philosophy is the basis of the film *Conan the Barbarian*, underlines the importance of metaphor in relation to the dominance of conceptual thinking. That's why he appreciates the arts, especially in the first phase of his work. In the second, weakest phase of his work, Nietzsche becomes a positivist who appreciates science, pushing the arts aside. Finally, in his third, most mature and fruitful phase of creation, Nietzsche considerably restores the importance of the arts, which he has previously diminished. After all, he himself is an artist as much as a philosopher. As the master of the aphorism, which is his hallmark and the great stylist, who shows his talent in *Thus Spoke Zarathustra*, Nietzsche keeps a reader's attention by artistic impression as much as by his ideas.

Knowing through the metaphor of an object of knowledge is the basic way of knowing. We learn the physical world through phenomenon. If we agree that there's *thing –in–itself* (we're using Kant's expression), then the phenomena are metaphors of some transcendent, unknowable world.

Let's get back to drawing the viewer into the world of some work of art. The ancient Greeks didn't have a problem to define the artist's vision of the world. Zeus, Apollo, Athens, Odysseus, Helen of Troy or Cassandra are well-known references to Greek consumers of works of art. Each of those references has characteristics that the artist can use in his work without having to define them previously. However, Milius has to define a world that only few people know. *Conan the Barbarian* is also created for someone, who is unfamiliar with Robert E Howard's work or the life in the Iron Age. He also wants to introduce Nietzsche's "overman", in the way, which would be attractive for someone who knows nothing about *Übermensch*. Here, to define means to create something so that something else can be built on it. Howard and Milius manage to create the world where the action of the movie will be set. Their effort should be appreciated more than the effort of modern artists since they were creating in the period without the Internet, when information was far more difficult to get. Particularly impressive is the fact that Milius first wanted to make a movie about Genghis Khan, but he almost unnoticeably and very successfully switched to the Cimmerian. But he deliberately left a trace about his original plan. The name of the thief and archer, who Conan rescues and who becomes his loyal friend is Subotai, like Genghis Khan's greatest general.

Let's leave Milius's intentions aside for now and let's get back to the movie itself. First, we'll see how the story unfolds, emphasizing what's important to us along the way. We'll pay attention to Conan's family. It's clear from the beginning that Conan comes from a high social class. At that time, a blacksmith was a well-paid and respectful job. Especially if you knew what the competition didn't. While most of them were still using bronze,

Conan's father was able to make long swords from iron. Iron, i.e. steel weapons are lighter than those made from bronze. Also, bronze, which is an alloy of copper and tin, isn't as solid as steel, and steel, besides its strength, isn't so brittle that the swordsman would fear that his sword would break into two pieces during the fight (although it's possible; it used to happen in the fights earlier). True, depending on the technological process, an iron (steel) sword can be made stronger but harder or more elastic. Besides that, we have to mention that carbon is added to the iron (in that way it becomes sharper but harder), so it's more accurate to call it steel sword. Anyway, it's possible to make longer swords from iron than from bronze, which allows for stronger swing and greater impact force. Force of the blow is even more important if the enemy is armored. Anyhow, the technology of making iron weapons, and especially swords as weapon of the elite was crucial for fighting in the ancient times and further on.

In Conan's time, it was so important that the human prehistoric period was named after technological products of demiurge such as Conan's father. The famous word related to magic, abracadabra, was probably used to determine the length of particular processes in metal casting. In the absence of precise measuring instruments for time measuring, the passage of time during metal processing was measured by saying certain words. To an impartial person, that would look like as if a blacksmith had been a wizard who, using certain magic formulas, did what he did. That wasn't far from the truth. The connection between magic and metallurgy was created in that prehistoric period and it continued as alchemy through the Middle Ages until modern times and modern science. In the arts, that connection is present even nowadays. After all, the epic fiction genre in the West is sometimes referred to as sword and sorcery genre.

At the beginning of the film, Conan's father assures his son of the quality of his products, including the whole craftsmen association. While telling him the myth of Chromos, who is Conan's, as shown later in the movie, mostly useless God (logically related to the mountain where the metals are mined), his father assures him of man's capabilities. Man is able to discover some secrets, which are reserved only for gods. That must have stuck in the mind of the young barbarian, given his strong will and disrespect, which he shows later for the demigod Doom.

He also assures him that he mustn't trust either man or woman (the latter may be crucial for the development of a healthy man), or beast, but an iron sword. True, it's a quite simple and humble but practical life philosophy.

Immediately after this educational story follows the attack on the village that really looks like a village from the Metal Ages. The horsemen are equally convincing, but those scenes aren't just historically convincing. There's an artistic credibility that other films of that genre don't possess. Already a sequel to *Conan the Barbarian*, *Conan the Destroyer* is made badly. At the beginning of that second movie, we can see a riding scene where the camera remains for too long at one spot, shooting the horse's head. The scene gets boring.   We'll discuss later about the other shortcomings. The above mentioned is just an illustration. There is also a Russian movie (*Wolfhound of The Grey Hound Clan*) that looks like a copy of *Conan the Barbarian*, where at the beginning of the movie they also attack the village, kill the boy's parents, etc. But those scenes don't have the power which Milius's movie has. Milius's horsemen ride through the woods as if history is just about to pull the young Cimmerian into its main course. The statics of the trees in the forest, through which the horsemen ride, creates the contrast that contributes to the dynamics of the whole scene of the attack on the village. In the scene where little Conan becomes aware of the attack, he has the visual contact with a warrior climbing a nearby rock. That warrior's appearance radiates savagery. Measured on the scale of evolution, he looks like being a step away from the animal. After irradiating the space with his savagery, the warrior stands up on the rock he has stepped on, and a bunch of horsemen surround him on each side, adding to the impression of danger and signaling the drama that follows. The above mentioned warrior is painted in the colors characteristic of the already mentioned Picts, the Celtic people, whose descendants are, at least partly, today's Scots.

From the beginning of the film until the mill scene, music by Basil Poledouris is truly *royal*, which we could have predicted based on the composer's name. Music is a master creation that carries masterpieces of picture and story. That splendid achievement of one of the five officially recognized arts is the essence of the first twenty minutes of the movie. Although the music is at its highest by the end of the movie, the beginning is so important for the impression and relationship you build with the story, the actors, their appearances and the scenery that it's difficult to imagine any other composition. It's as if Basil was possessed by the same demon[5] that haunted Milius. It seems as if that demon acted, by pulling the strings, through both of them at the same time.

The very first sounds in the movie resemble a thunderstorm announcing the arrival of a storm. The theme of the movie sounds like the sound of the essence of the epic perception of the world. It was as if Basil was a disguised pan, not a composer, who wasn't satisfied with the instruments available to the class of pans, so he decided to use the musical evolution of man and the trumpets, drums and lyres that man created. Basil is a pan that challenges the gods with his skill. The choir he uses announces tragedy in the same way his tribal ancient ancestor announced tragedy in works dealing with heroes of Greek myth. Here, the choir is also a part of the fate, *ananka*[6], which announces to its victim what follows, regardless of whether the victim is Conan's village or Dart Vader with a face. However, with the music, that tragedy nurtures its dignity, draws us into the battle, makes us participate with our hearts if not with our bodies. It draws some childlike naivety out of us, the desire of a male child to be a famous warrior. The forests

---

[5] In ancient Greek meaning of the word- guiding spirit, provider of destiny- not from today horror genre.

[6] A goddess in Greek mythology, a personification of destiny

and mountains of Cimmeria look like inhospitable, cold forests and mountains of Hyperborea to us. The music of Poledeuris makes Conan's mother look even more dignified and Thulsa Doom even more mysterious. The rattle of metal, the cries of the dying, the whistling of swords cutting through the air are perfect sections that fit with Basil's theme, the will of the above mentioned demon that possessed him and Milius. That creates the harmony between image, note and natural, undisciplined sound. Only demons can tell the true story of gods and heroes. Demons possessed rhapsodists and other poets, giving them inspiration. Can anyone doubt that Homer was possessed by a demon? There's a connection between the artist and the world that's hidden from other people, regardless of what Nietzsche thought about metaphysics and other worlds. For a moment, Basil was a part of that transcendent place, filled with artistic essence, which, although it gives its immaterial structure to rare lucky people (which is what we call inspiration), loses nothing of its essentiality.

In his early days, Nietzsche admired Schopenhauer as a philosopher and Wagner as an artist. For Nietzsche, Wagner is the ideal of an artist, while Schopenhauer is the ideal of a philosopher. Nietzsche used to be friends with Wagner for a while. He believed that Wagner had some characteristics of a hero, which helped him overcome the demonic nature from which artists draw their inspiration. The product of the struggle between demons and heroes that resided in Wagner's spirit are his works of art. Wagner is the creator of a new style in the arts, but even more he's a restorer of mythology, a faithful representative of the eternal motives of life and what's also interesting for us, he's also an interesting creator of the unity of music and drama. Friedrich Nietzsche believed that Schopenhauer's philosophy, which he considered the most truthful at the time, spoke through Wagner's music. No wonder Nietzsche admired Wagner so much in that early age of his development. He considered the arts more valuable than truth. The illusion, fantasy, deception embodied in the arts is deeper and more original than truth, reality and being. In fact, our will wants illusion instead of truth.

Before Nietzsche, no one supported the arts so strongly. Let's remind us, how much Plato, by far the most significant philosopher of all time, isn't the biggest fan of artists. He believes that artists are inspired by demonic power but in fact, they don't really know what they're talking about. Of course, he's referring to rhapsodists and poets like Homer and Hesiod. His opinion of fine arts is even worse. Painting is a copy of a copy. While a material thing is a copy of an immaterial, indestructible idea of that thing, a painting has an even lower ontological status because it's a representation of a copy. Plato is a philosopher to whom truth and knowledge are essential to man's relationship with the world. He criticizes poets for the following reasons: in traditional Greek society, poets enjoyed the status of the nation's teachers. Education and upbringing were carried out according to the values set by the poetry art embodied in Homer. Plato believed that poets shouldn't be shown respect, which they were enjoying, since they lacked knowledge. After all, would you trust your child's education today to someone who doesn't know what he's talking about? Plato saw the poets, Homer in the first place, as his competition. Aristocles wanted education to be based on knowledge, whose example we follow by doing the same nowadays. Although he spared the music criticism for its importance for the development of the soul in his elaboration of an ideal society (*The Republic*), the rulers of the republic create their legitimacy based on the knowledge they possess. It's interesting that the examples which Plato gives as bad for the upbringing of the young, and which he thinks should be censored, Nietzsche would reject too. In the first place, those are the words of Achilles, whom Odysseus[7] meets in Hades:

> By god, I'd rather slave on earth for another man--/
> Some dirt-poor tenant farmer who scrapes to keep alive—

---

[7] Plato gives the example from *Odysseus*

than rule down here over all the breathless dead."

Liefer were I in the fields up above to be serf to another
Tiller of some poor plot which yields him a scanty subsistence,
Than to be ruler and king over all the dead who have perished,
Lest unto men and immortals the homes of the dead be
uncovered
Horrible, noisome, dank, that the gods too hold in abhorrence,
Ah me! So it is true that e'en in the dwellings of Hades
Spirit there is and wraith, but within there is no understanding,
Sole to have wisdom and wit, but the others are shadowy
phantoms,
Forth from his limbs unwilling his spirit flitted to Hades,
Wailing its doom and its lustihood lost and the May of its
manhood,

Under the earth like a vapor vanished the gibbering soul,
Even as bats in the hollow of some mysterious grotto
Fly with a flitter mouse shriek when one of them falls from the
cluster
Whereby they hold to the rock and are clinging the one to the
other,
Flitted their gibbering ghosts.[8]

Such Achilles' complaining certainly doesn't suit someone who is considered to be the greatest hero of *The Iliad*, who had the possibility to choose between immortality and mortality and chose the latter, opposing the will of the gods. The very choice he made is the essence of his heroism. If it hadn't been for that, Achilles wouldn't have been a hero, considering the invulnerability of his body, with the exception of his heel. Surely, Nietzsche would also reject such arts, which presents the hero as someone who whines

---

[8]From 386c to 387a taken from
http://www.perseus.tufts.edu/hopper/text?doc=Perseus%3Atext%3A19
99.01.0168%3Abook%3D3%3Asection%3D386c

about his fate stemming from his own heroic choice. Unfortunately, there's something similar in an original version of *Conan the Barbarian*. After Conan's sweetheart dies, when Conan and his friends are preparing for the arrival of Thulsa Doom and his warriors, there's a scene where Conan and Subotai talk and Conan complains about his fate. That whining doesn't suit "overman", Conan's artistic ideal. Fortunately, in the shorter version of the movie, that scene was deleted. For technical reasons, some scenes were cut when the movie was first released in DVD format. Apart from that scene, scenes with the princess at the end of the movie were deleted too. In the original version of the movie, Conan goes away with the princess toward the horizon, carrying her in his arms the way a groom caries a bride over the threshold and all of that happens at dawn. Luckily, that Hollywood tackiness was deleted in the shorter version. The shorter version seems more realistic, considering everything we know about Conan and Nietzsche. So, in case you haven't watched the movie so far, we recommend the shorter version.

As we could notice from the above, both Plato and Nietzsche need a hero. Plato needs a hero to be the guardian of an ideal community. The ideal community consists of three classes. The first one is a class of producers made up of craftsmen and farmers; the second one is a class of guards, warriors who need to fight for the good of the community, while at the top is the class of leaders, recruited by the selection between the best guards. The tripartite division of the state is related to Plato's division of the soul into three parts. One part is the appetitive part, which is related to passions, which we can consider lower. Also, there is an urge to drink and eat. The virtue of that part of the soul is moderation. The next, higher part (from *thymos* - heart, heartiness, courage) is in line with something which we would call will nowadays. That part is related to higher passions. For example, the thirst for glory is the passion characteristic of that part of the soul. Timocracy, a form of government, which arises when the ideal community begins to fail, and people as a major value, have the desire to compete, to celebrate, to hunt, to prove. The virtue of that part of the soul is courage. That part of the soul is in many ways oriented towards others and therefore it isn't independent. We'll deal with the problems of will later, but here, we have to mention that, according to some, the Greeks didn't perceive will the way we talk about it nowadays. The third aspect of the soul, which can be mostly aligned with the class of leaders in the ideal community, is the rational part of the soul. Its virtue is wisdom, rationality. Ratio is the characteristic of that part of the soul. When those parts, i.e. aspects of the soul, are in line, soul is in harmony, possessing health that's value itself. Heroism, which we're interested in, is a trait of a warrior class in an ideal community.

With Nietzsche, things are different. Heroism is value by itself. We don't need anything beyond that. Heroic life is meaningful and gives value to the world. With early Nietzsche, while he was still in the shadow of Schopenhauer and Wagner, the artistic genius was a hero. Everything is subordinated to the art that lives through its genius. It's important to notice that Nietzsche already at his beginning turns to the irrational. Schopenhauer's philosophy is the philosophy of the irrational, whiles the arts, regardless of form, is again the matter of irrationality, regardless whether we talk about inspiration or talent. Neither inspiration nor talent can be explained by rational means. Later, Nietzsche will make a step backwards, by becoming a positivist, a man of science, moving the arts from the pedestal, where he placed it. Perhaps that phase was created under the influence of changes in personal attitude towards Wagner. Nietzsche distanced from his former role model. It was probably because the two geniuses couldn't stand each other. Nietzsche needed solitude. After the period of love of science and being a positivist, which wasn't that fruitful, Nietzsche will once again return to the irrational in his mature creative age, which is the most important for his oeuvre.

Nowadays, when we think of Wagner, the first association is his work *Ride of the Valkyries.* That music was used in the film classic *Apocalypse Now* by Francis Ford Coppola (Millius was a screenwriter). Members of the US Air Force are using it in the attack on the Viet Cong. The movie portrays a helicopter attack on a Vietnamese village with those epic Dionysian notes. Nietzsche would have certainly liked a scene like that. He would have probably liked to hear Basil Poledouris's notes even more. He believed that Schopenhauer's philosophy, which was for young Nietzsche the highest and most true, spoke through Wagner's music. Nietzsche's philosophy speaks through Basil's music. Although Basil had other successes, such as *Robocop* and *The Hunt for Red October*, he will be remembered for the composition he created for *Conan the Barbarian*. Poledouris expresses a raw, freed, Dionysian force, which celebrates heroes, but which is finely artistically polished and refined in the Apollonian notes' order, a rational invention that opposes it but also complements the Dionysian.

In Nietzsche's terminology, *Conan the Barbarian* combines the Dionysian urge for destruction, darkness, chaos, strength and depth with an Apollonian sense of order, harmony and beauty. The fight between those two urges results in tragedy in Greek art. Tragedy is Greek understanding of the world. It isn't some sentimental pessimism that sees misery and sadness everywhere; it expands to deeper of the world through human action, which is always limited by some higher power, fate, necessity, will of the gods. Nietzsche believed that the arts are a metaphysical consolation. According to him, tragedy isn't a story but an action. It's interesting that young Conan in the movie doesn't say anything. The chronicler speaks for him. Young Conan acts, although his actions are reduced to getting impressions until the mill scene. The way you interpret your impressions is also action. Conan doesn't turn his eyes away from the horrid scene of his father's death. His mother doesn't cover his eyes at that moment. She gave birth to the hero. That mother is the exact opposite of many mothers today who are just trying to make their children's lives easier and protect them from suffering. Young Conan is silent even when Thulsa Doom kills her and when he loses her. Until the end, she shows her maternal instinct (and Nietzsche appreciates instinct more than knowledge) in protecting her baby. However, her instinct isn't enough to prepare her to fight against the will of Thulsa Doom -the will, which he uses together with suggestion to break spiritual resistance, instincts, and the will of other beings. Will is another thing that Nietzsche appreciates even more than instinct. After all, the will to power is basically everything. The will to power, which that creature has, is even stronger than maternal instinct. After all, isn't maternal instinct only a disguised desire to overcome the limitations of human existence, a hidden manifestation of the will to power?

Anyway, Conan loses maternal protection and love. The scene where Conan's mom is ready to fight the attackers although the battle is already lost, testifies to the irrational essence of human nature. The appearance of Thulsa's Dukes and Doom himself also shows us logic of the irrational. Unlike the armor and helmets of Roman legionnaires or medieval armor, which, with few exceptions, were rationally designed, Thulsa Doom and his warriors have irrationally made helmets. Their helmets are more works of art than usable items. They have ornaments. Rexor has a helmet with long ornaments, which look like stylized horns. Thulsa Doom appears with a helmet decorated with snakes looking at each other. The lower part of Doom's helmet reminds of helmet in classical Greece. Leonidas's Spartans wore something similar. The upper part is his personal mark, an emblem, which is in line with his nature. He, Doom, follows some sort of heraldic urge in creating his defensive weapon. Again something irrational.

On the other hand, the curvature and shape of the armor are the product of rational thinking and experience. If a weapon hits you, it's better if it hit sat an angle as steep as possible, which is less than ninety degrees. The blow is the strongest at ninety-degree angle. That's why sloped, rounded armor is more durable than straight, cubic armor with protruding parts. The chances are greater to survive the blow if there are fewer protruding parts and if the armor is more rounded and sleeker. That's rational. That rational logic is timeless. Sloped armor is thicker when hit at ninety-degree angle. In the development of walls of European fortifications, i.e. fortified cities, at a time when firearms emerged and evolved, embodied in cannon artillery and bombards. Logic necessarily led to the construction of sloped fortified walls. If we look at the engravings of fortified cities from the 18th century, we'll see series of sloped walls constructed in the way that wherever they received a hit it should be, geometrically, at most possible distance from ninety degrees. The idea is to reject the projectiles.

However, Thulsa's men, as well as the historical "Sea Peoples", called like that by the ancient Egyptians, who were exposed to the conquest by those people at one point in history; don't believe that such understanding plays a major role in making armor. Those with armor, decorated with metal ornaments, are self-confident. They don't worry about receiving a hit; they're dealing with how to strike an opponent. Their aesthetics should signal the opponent to run while he still can. Fear is the feeling, they want to extract from their enemies. It's a rational logic that has irrational urges for its base. The snakes on top of Doom's helmet are spiritually connected with the snakes that make up Medusa's hair. Another reason, of course, is the desire to be special, to stand out from the masses and to show one's privileged position.

In the scene where Thulsa Doom appears in front of Conan and his mother, one should also bear in mind that extra dose of fear he injects into the bodies, and even more into the souls of his victims. Thus Conan, in a very violent and psychologically striking way, loses his protector and provider. We have to mention one more thing regarding the scene where Conan becomes an orphan. Besides that powerful scene by Milius, it's recommended to see another scene, which is a work of art for the simple reason of being a fine art that is static in its nature. There's a difference between the arts since some are static and others are dynamic. Painting and sculpture are static arts and their expression is different from dynamic arts like poetry or film. This has its advantages and disadvantages. In my opinion, work by Uros Predic "An Orphan upon His Mother's Grave" is more powerful in its expression and it manages to portray better the horror of loss and the coldness of the world in such a situation. Although he isn't as good at expression as Predic, Milius manages to bring closer even greater Conan's loss. Not only does Conan lose his father and his mother, he also loses his people. We should bear in mind that a child from such a village and from that period in history, i.e. prehistory, had the world reduced to the stories of adults and the physical environment of the village. Unlike children today who receive lots of information through mass media and communication, and who can get a broader, if not deeper understanding of the world and by interacting with a large number of people, little Conan has only his village. The shock he experienced with the attack on his small world could be only compared to some catastrophe of the planetary proportions of today's world. Thulsa Doom took everything away from Conan but his bare life. Among other things, the beginning of *Conan the Barbarian* is a disaster movie. Disaster, which isn't just symptomatic of the Iron Age. The truth is that, besides the events happening in the Cimmeria forest shown in the movie, the historical and archeological evidence is full of similar events. In Tacitus' *Germania*, various tribes were mentioned, nations that had experienced a cruel fate. Interestingly, Tacitus also mentioned some Celts who were excellent in making weapons but they forgot to use them, so a Germanic tribe enslaved them, to produce good weapons for them.

It turned out in a dramatic and violent way that in the twentieth century an ordinary man couldn't live in the luxury of being interested only in trivial matters. The course of events in the world doesn't leave anyone behind, not even the most backward and remote cultures. During the Pacific War, even the most isolated tribes got in touch with the Eastern performance of the world mainstream, the war between the Japanese and the Allies.

What can some European expect then? An ordinary man can't escape the world course. No matter what we do, historical processes will draw us into their mechanism, into their grinder, which grinds human destinies, and one should be prepared for it. One can't hope that all will be well in the end. Man must prepare for the worst. After all, in which end? In grave? Even so, according to our philosopher of the irrational, one should enjoy life, because no matter how painful it is, pleasure is so big that it nullifies all the pain.

A FIGHT FOR RECOGNITION

Did it ever happen to you when you were a child that some other children snatch your toy, soccer ball, bicycle, doll, skateboard, t-shirt, purse or sneakers? If you were the victim of such an unpleasant event, maybe somewhere in the depths of your soul, besides the sorrow for the alienated material things, you also felt the emotional pain for not being respected as a person. If you have felt such emotional pain at least once in your life, then it'll be easier for you to understand one Hegel's idea, which is the basis of the plot of *"Conan the Barbarian"*. One of the main Barbarian's motives isn't just a mere desire for vengeance, but a desire for recognition as well.

Above mentioned Hegel's idea emerged as a competition against the concepts of social atomism. Social atomism, which is the characteristic of the Western philosophy of the Modern period and contemporary era, seemed to be insufficient for Hegel to explain the inclusion of individuals in social relations. Even Machiavelli earlier created an image of the society, which is taken to be understood as the struggle of individuals for resources. Despite the fact that Machiavelli has dealt with the struggle of higher classes, potential rulers in fact, the author of *The Prince* doesn't deal with ordinary people particularly, except when the support of that people is an instrument of coming to power and preserving it. From the context of his work, we can discern the concept of society where rules war of all against all. Basically, the ruler endeavors to direct the energy of uninterrupted conflicts among people in an intelligent way and for his own benefit. There's one theoretically unexplained but implicitly present metaphysical assumption in Machiavelli's writings: that the field of social action is the continuous interaction of subjects for the preservation of physical identity, or to put it in simple language - the most important activity of people is the tendency to remain alive as long as possible.

Some 120 years after Machiavelli, an English philosopher had the privilege of being born in an epistemically favorable age to establish a philosophical, scientifically based thesis on the all against all war. Hobbes believed that people are basically self-propelled mechanisms, whose specificity lies in their ability to care for their well-being in the future. Thomas Hobbes argued that when two people meet, the feature of each person to care for his own good in the future creates a kind of preventive escalation of power that's born out of suspicion. Since both subjects have to stay unknown and incomprehensible in their intentions to each other, they're both working on increasing their potentials in terms of power, training for some future defense against the possible attacks of the other person.

Hobbes was born the same year when England was frightened by the attack of the Spanish Armada (1588). Under the leadership of Sir Francis Drake and Queen Elizabeth, England managed to defend itself from that menace, although the chances weren't in favor of England. The survival of Protestantism, which contributed to the formation of modern English identity, is the main consequence of naval triumph over Spain. The victory of Spain would also mean the victory of the papacy. In spite of the avoidance of foreign invasion of people of another religion, England in the next - the 17th century, found itself in nothing less historical disaster.

According to many people, civil war is the worst thing that can hit one nation. That was exactly what happened to the English. The war began with a conflict between the king and Parliament. King Charles I Stewart stubbornly insisted on the right of kings to absolute power. That brought him into conflict with Parliament, which naturally insisted on a consensus between the King and Parliament. The stubbornness of King Charles I brought him to the executioner who cut his head off following the court order of Parliament.

As shown in the above mentioned, the English were about 150 years ahead of the French on this issue. French guillotine was just a technical progress. The idea that Parliament can cut off the head of a king is an Anglo-Saxon invention thanks to English political avant-garde. However, the French, whose country has more sunny days, reached more easily the state of mind whose appropriate term would be the expression *"hot brained"*, and who couldn't stop until they cut off a few dozens of heads of ordinary citizens as well as some heads of the leaders of the revolution. And then how can someone say that there is no progress? Not only did the development of technical sciences enable the industrialization of head cutting, but the French Revolution allowed everyone to remain headless regardless social status, sex, age or real guilt.

The English Civil War continued on several occasions. At one time, England was a republic, and that was the only time in history. English President Oliver Kromwell, with the title Lord Protector, was taken out of grave after his death and his corpse was dragged through the streets of London. It seems that the English have been born as monarchists. The conflict between Royalists and Parliamentarians ended with the replacement of the Stuart dynasty, which, by the way, was Catholic and Scottish. Parliament managed to win a far greater limitation of royal power, and the new King, William of Orange, was a Protestant. Life was very cruel in the period of the English Civil War. Besides those who were killed in fights, many people died from contagious diseases, such as plague, starvation, and many prisoners were sold as slaves and ended up outside the British Isles. Although the Civil War was in England, Ireland, which lost about 40% of the population, is the biggest victim.

Such images of a permanent war have led Thomas Hobbes to articulate the idea of a natural state. The natural state is the state of interpersonal relations where there are no social institutions. There's a constant fight between people for basic needs in it. Since there are no rights, there's no injustice either. In such a state, there isn't place for any work, culture or society. Man's life is solitary, poor, nasty, brutish, and short. Natural state rules, i.e. the freedom that every person does everything he can to sustain himself in life with his own powers. This includes the freedom to kill or steal to get food. Hobbes believes that people are born equal because no one is strong enough to defend himself from another person independently. Everyone can be killed on sleep or may be overpowered by several people who have joined.

Actually, Hobbes is discussing the issues of political philosophy that were sharply highlighted at that time: Why do some people have the right to rule over others? What's the origin of social institutions? Do people have some natural rights? Where does the individual's consent with the principles of a particular political community come from? These questions differ from the ancient understanding of political problems. We're all familiar with Aristotle's claim that there can be only a beast or God outside society and a man is a social being. Aristotle, without distinguishing himself regarding that idea from the other main political philosopher of the ancient era - Plato, believes in the primacy of community. Polis has priority over the individual. Happiness or moral virtue can't be found outside community. The political theory of those two most important philosophers of ancient times is moving in the direction of finding the best possible arrangement to which individuals must succumb. Plato is more extreme than Aristotle. He believes that one part of society has no right to property, while the other part has almost insurmountable obstacles in case it wants to be educated, and all that for the sake of harmony of the whole community.

After the awakening of human rationality in the Renaissance and the rejection of ecclesiastical dogmas about the world and man, some philosophers tried to answer questions related to the functioning of human society, which were dating from the ancient era. Times and customs has changed so much since the ancient times that all attempts were unsuccessful. With

Machiavelli and Hobbes, new political ideas were born. The community loses its priority, and the individual becomes more important than the whole. The society now consists of individuals, who, according to Hobbes, can't pass from their natural state into the state of law and rights due to logical reasons. Since the person who attacks first in the relationship between two people has priority, individuals themselves can by no means get out of their natural state. Why should they stick to the agreement when the one who breaks it first gains advantage? Those who are more interested in it can relate the situation of individuals in natural state with the dilemma of prisoners in the game theory.

In order to overcome that problem, Hobbes introduces the institution of omnipotent sovereign. The one, who's powerful enough to secure the respect of the agreement by force and fear, has the right to rule. His subordinates entrust their rights to him in exchange for the protection and securing the peace. Hobbes didn't think that there was really a situation in the past without any institutions, although the era of civil war was very similar to a natural state. His goal was to solve the philosophical problems that we've mentioned: what's the origin of political institutions and what do they base their legitimacy on? We can see that the idea of providing protection isn't without historical background in many cases of the synthesis of warrior aristocracy and the productive part of the population. After all, besides Conan's Thraco - Cimmerians, there's such an example in the English society itself. After the battle of Hastings in 1066, the Norman nobility replaced the Anglo-Saxon aristocracy. Nothing much changed for ordinary people, although in the beginning it was more difficult for the Saxons under foreign rule. Once the new authority was established, the provision of protection remained the basic function of the Norman nobility. The aristocracy of the ancient Greek Athenian society probably descended from the protection groups as well. The origin of Italian mafia also shows us how important the function of protection is for mere functioning of society. The mafia was formed in the south of Italy, when the state was collapsing and it couldn't fulfill its protector function.

Locke and Rousseau have believed in the idea of a social contract according to which previously socially atomized individuals form society. They've been further developing and adapting that idea to social conditions. Individuals acquire some rights by birth, and those rights have been guaranteed for the first time by the US Constitution and the Charter of Rights. In Europe, those rights have been introduced to the great extent with the French Revolution and legal norms proceeded from it. Nowadays, human rights have become *sacred* in the politics of Western democracies, and thus under the pretext of protecting human rights, we've reached the concept of "humanitarian" military intervention.

To summarize: In ancient times, there was an idea of the priority of polis over citizens' rights; nowadays, society is being built from the primacy of individuals over social organizations. What bothered Hegel in his early period is more or less a mechanistic way of constituting a society in a modern philosophical thought. According to him, there's an external, unnatural force. Hegel's trying to overcome that problem by seeking the way to explain the creation of social institutions in a more organic and natural way. Encouraged by Fichte, Hegel's been developing the idea of recognition. Fichte's believed that recognition is the mutual interrelation of individuals, and that it's the basis of legal relations. People are asking each other to act freely while at the same time, they're limiting their scope of activities to benefits of the other person. Subjects create common awareness, which is objectively valid in legal relations.

Hegel believes that a subject's ready to reconcile with the other subject to that extent to which he knows that another subject will acknowledge some of his qualities and abilities. The subject through the other person partially discovers his own separate identity, which opposes to that other subject as something individual. Within the commonly established mutual recognition, subjects always learn something new about their personal identity. In those relationships, they see how a certain dimension of their self is confirmed. Through the conflict, they're leaving the regular level, which they have achieved, in order to gain recognition of more demanding form of their individuality. The recognition process, which forms the basis of common (moral) relationship between the subjects, consists of a gradual sequence of alternate reconciliations and conflicts. In this way, Hegel is solving the problem that exists in atomistic construction of the world. Every person needs other people to build their own identity. In a particular historical moment, subjects are forced to leave and overcome the common relationships where they've found themselves just because they believe that in those relationships their individual identity hasn't received a satisfactory recognition. The conflict that arises isn't just because of physical survival as Machiavelli and Hobbes believe. Besides basic means for bare life, a person wants to be recognized to the level he personally thinks he deserves. Let's get back to the English case. They refused to be inferior regarding their own language. Why would they allow the monopoly of Latin and Greek when it comes to using Scripture or church rituals? Isn't English good enough to communicate with God? By the rebellion against the Pope, the English fought for a new position in the mutual recognition with Rome. They first received recognition by moving from paganism to Christianity. However, at some point in history that wasn't enough anymore. Since the Tudor period[9], they started desiring their own church as well, political independence from the Pope. They needed a new level of recognition. What Hegel considers important regarding the term *recognition* (and regarding that he differs even more from Machiavelli and Hobbes) is his opinion that identity is more important than life. A person with strong personality is capable of endangering his life and all that he possesses to win the level of recognition he thinks he deserves – i.e. he wants to be identified in

---

[9] I don't deny other reasons, especially personal reasons of King Henry VIII

the eyes of the other person according to high standards he attributes to himself.

The English were ready to fight against the superior opponent and risk their lives for their identity. Their civil war can be interpreted from this position as well. In English society, there were those who defended the right of kings to absolute power, extending their argumentation to Adam's period and the creation of man. From the point of view of those philosophers, Parliament committed a crime when it convicted and executed King Charles I. According to Hegel, the source of the crime is precisely an incomplete recognition. The inner urge of the criminal lies in his experience of not being recognized in a satisfactory manner at the established stage of mutual recognition. The King didn't want to recognize the right of Parliament to rule by restricting his will by mutual consensus. There was a fight for recognition. The King, i.e. the personality of Charles Stuart I, couldn't allow the erosion of his power, because in that way his identity would change. He would no longer be what he was. By choosing death rather than yield, he did exactly what Hegel has predicted in theory. Recognition from others, i.e. society, is more important than our own life. Parliamentarians were also ready to go to the end. They no longer wanted to be in a secondary social position in relation to the institution and the personality of the King. Those are the Hegelian metaphysical causes of civil war - the struggle for recognition or acknowledgment from the others that we are worth as much as we value ourselves. An additional motive for the war was the identity of the English themselves. The Stuarts were Catholics, while the English nation has been building its identity precisely on opposing to Catholicism. The legal norms, which are valid even today, speak the most of how far the English were ready to go in preserving their identity. The King of England must not be a Catholic or marry a Catholic (Meanwhile, there have been changes since the Serbian edition of this book, which is unusual, since the monarch is also the head of the Church of England). Let's get back to the example of the snatched toy from the beginning of this chapter. The mental pain that you've suffered comes from the fact that your personality hasn't been recognized. The attacker doesn't recognize you as a person equal to himself. If you accept the fight, and according to Hegel, that's the only appropriate answer, you're the one who treats himself as a person with integrity. You are fighting for the integrity of your whole self, while the (snatcher) criminal is satisfying some of his individual interests. The attacked subject must win the fight because he takes that personally, as the offence of his whole personality. The conflict isn't based on the violation of individual pretensions to a certain right (in this case property right), but in violation of the integrity of the person as a whole. Hegel calls this battle a battle for honor, where the honor is the attitude you take towards yourself. Fight for honor is necessary because such affirmative attitude towards oneself depends on the recognition from other people. When two people are aiming to re-establish their honor, and trying to convince the other person that their personality deserves recognition, convincing will succeed only if they show to each other that they're ready to sacrifice their lives. According to Hegel, only by being willing to die, I show publicly that my individual goals and characteristics are more important than my physical survival. Thus, Hegel allows the social conflict, which occurs as a consequence of an insult, to turn into a fight for life or death, a fight that can't be legally explained since it concerns the whole person and it goes beyond the limits which law can define. In our case, from childhood when we fight for the toy, we let the snatcher know that he must see us as a person, not as a way of satisfying his needs. The fight for recognition builds our identity.

In that way, conflicts produce morally more mature methods of recognition. Through each new challenge entailed by various crimes, either their own or those of the others, people always gain additional knowledge of their own and unique identity. A whole person is the one establishing recognition of its own uniqueness whereas an ordinary person establishes only a legal status. Over time, the fight for honor develops in the fight of entire communities. Human spirit that helps the development of consciousness needs to know that others recognize it and it can know it only through conflict. A strong person gets a cognitive confirmation from other people in interaction only if he's experienced other people's reaction to targeted provocation. Therefore, conflict is a way of social integration because we can't develop our own consciousness and personal integrity without the reactions and acknowledgments of others.

In his philosophy, Hegel later neglects his idea of recognition in favor of speculation on the development of consciousness. An important detail refers to the creation of works, as a product of one's activity mediated by the use of tools. Thanks to his work, the subject becomes aware that he's able to constitute reality, and that the subject himself has created the content of that reality. While awareness of the world was merely cognitive, it couldn't know its power to change reality. That change of reality can happen only under the pressure of self-discipline. By noticing the results of his work, the spirit of a particular subject sees himself as a being capable of activity thanks to self-control. That reminds of Nietzsche and his ideas of self-esteem, but in fact, we can notice the beginning of Marx's philosophy in those Hegel's ideas.

In *Conan the Barbarian,* the Cimmerian is in an interesting situation where he literally creates himself. After the children from his village have been enslaved, the Barbarian spends his youth turning the mill. He doesn't see much world geographically and he doesn't develop cognitively in the sense where cognition means gathering information. However, he learns something even more important. He learns that the world can be changed and it can be changed in the way that suites him. Unlike other children, who die one by one over time, (which is only indicated by Milius's artistic metaphors), Conan creates his body using his will and the body just as a tool. Although he has grown up as a slave, the Cimmerian builds his consciousness and his will by realizing that he can change and create a new reality. That psychological state is of utmost importance for the venture that's growing in Conan's personality since the murder of his family and genocide of his people. The event that's taken away his family, people and childhood is the moment when the Cimmerian begins to build his identity. He can only react to that crime by accepting the fight. The core of the Barbarian's personality, which he builds and shows through the whole film, is that everyone, no matter how powerful he is, has to respect him. His relationship with Thulsa Doom isn't based solely on mere revenge, but also on the desire for recognition. Conan isn't anyone and he can't be treated in the way he's been treated, no matter if it comes to Thulsa Doom or history itself. Conan respects himself, and he's ready to pay the highest price. What's life without the recognition of him as a person? This can be seen also in the part of the film when he fights in the arena where he begins to realize his true value. Conan manages to gain the recognition of the audience with his gladiatorial battle to death. Although that recognition is incomplete, it's of great importance. It gives the Barbarian's personality extra security. Thus, Milius suggests the solution to the problem that lies in the relationship between a master and a slave (servant). Kojève[10] dealt with that famous Hegelian problem regarding recognition.

When two people meet for the first time, they're trying to impose their will and their self on the other person. For that reason, a fight develops and the winner is frustrated in any outcome. If he kills an opponent he wins the fight itself, but he doesn't receive recognition because the opponent would rather die than subordinates his self to another person and recognizes him as a more worthy master. On the other hand, if the defeated, faced with the choice between death and recognition of power to the winner, surrender and fall into slavery, or service, the winner remains denied in recognition. He's been recognized by a weak

---

[10] Alexandre Kojève was a French philosopher who greatly influenced 20th-century French philosophy. He integrated Hegelian concepts into twentieth-century continental philosophy.

person who isn't worth enough because he hasn't been ready to give his life in a fight for the recognition of his identity.

In Conan's case, he receives recognition from a neutral but interested and qualified party. In a sense, recognition of the audience is true recognition. Let's quote Conan's chronicler: "He didn't care anymore. Life and death …the same…only that the crowd would be there to greet him with howls of lust and fury. He began to realize his sense of worth… he mattered" (He matters - he counts, he's valuable). Therefore, the Cimmerian, even though he's a slave, receives recognition. Perhaps it's a bit paradoxical, but we should take into account that Conan's become a slave as a child and he doesn't know for better. He isn't one of those theoretical cases when two men meet for the first time and they try to impose their own self to each other. The Barbarian's case is also paradoxical from the point of Marxism's view. That philosophical and ideological discourse is present (still) in many parts of our society and we mustn't neglect it. According to Marx, when products of human labor reach the market, they alienate from their creator. The work itself becomes alienated because the means of production aren't under the control of the worker. Conan's body is both the product of labor and means of labor, and it's in the hands of his slave-owner who acquires capital using the Cimmerian as a gladiator. Yet, it's hard to imagine that Conan feels alienated from his body. He feels his body in an epistemically privileged way and apart from the fact that the other people acknowledge it as a successful killing machine, no one else can feel his body in the way Conan feels it.

Regarding recognition, our identity – I mean the identity of writers (philosophers) - also depends on the recognition of audience. If this book doesn't satisfy an average educated reader I won't receive the desired recognition either. Unrecognized artist is an unsuccessful artist and there's nothing more to add here. There's no need to fight to death, the audience gives their judgment.

Besides honor, an important role in recognition plays also a sexual, i.e. *love recognition.* Sexuality is a form of unification of opposing subjects. Thus, sexuality becomes an important, although not the only, connective tissue of an atomized society. According to Hegel, in order to be acknowledged in love, we need to be able to see ourselves in another person. The development of the subject's personal recognition is related to the type of recognition, which he receives from other subjects. There's a problem with that type of recognition, because it seems that only the average persons can get the true recognition.

Let's imagine a beautiful girl, actually a gorgeous girl, extremely intelligent, well educated, cheerful and witty, a girl who comes from a "good family", wealthy, with impeccable manners in social behavior, with developed and personal style of dressing etc... altogether a very desirable girl. Such a girl, has been exposed to courting of the opposite sex since her childhood (and why not her own sex as well). At first glance, she's been gaining and confirming her sexual recognition over and over again. It's similar to the one that the Cimmerian gets from the audience. We have to mention that women doubt their beauty. In order to know that they're beautiful they need to get confirmation from others. It's interesting that many girls have high opinion of themselves concerning their beauty even without the confirmation of others. Thus, they can spend their life in that illusion. However, let's get back to our perfect girl. The problem, which that girl has from the Hegelian perspective (if we take into account our knowledge of sexes), is that there's no man who can give her recognition. Men and women have different sexual functions and goals. From an evolutionary point of view, the sexual act itself is much more problematic for women than for men. Even today, with so many different contraceptives, many people decide to have unsafe sexual intercourse, for the sake of greater pleasure. After all, contraceptives aren't perfect. For example, using pills that mess up hormones isn't a desirable choice for many women. Many other people decide not to use a condom in the initial phase of the intercourse to have more intense experience so they use it only after a certain time, and the risks of pregnancy are rising. From all of the above, we can conclude that even in today's society there's a certain possibility of unwanted pregnancy. In pre-scientific times, i.e. several generations ago, the incidence of unwanted pregnancy was very high. A single mother in a society without developed mechanism of social protection couldn't provide prospects for a happy life of her children. In the longest period of human evolution, a woman who would try to raise children without a man, who would help her and provide material resources, wouldn't have big chances of success when it comes to bare survival, let alone something else. Natural selection has created mechanisms of defense against unreasonable sexual intercourses in the vast majority of women. Those defense mechanisms aren't perfect and sometimes they give in to the temptation but they do exist. It's not in the interest of a woman, who has achieved an evolutionary success, to have a large number of sexual intercourses with different partners. The social status and power of sexual partners are more important.[11] In short, the formula for success is to have as few as possible quality men. A woman also has to try to bind emotionally a desirable man to herself so that she can use a successful man for a longer period. That's another addition to the formula of success.

From an evolutionary point of view, a man has completely opposite goals. Men who had sexual intercourses with a large number of women had the biggest chance to reproduce and transfer their genes. The quality of those women is important, but we're interested in the fact that the desire for a larger number of

---

[11] This changes a bit in societies with exceptionally emancipated women, especially if the state significantly mediates between men and women in terms of financial aid to single mothers, expensive divorces where mostly men are impoverished, etc. Then, like in the case of younger women, the man's beauty plays bigger role. The devastation created by state policy can be also seen in the fact that men are losing their will to get married, and women are striving more for hypergamy.

partners is what differentiates the male behavior and psychological constitution from those of women. Some "modern" women ask themselves: why is a man who has been with many women a cool guy, and a woman who has been with many men a s..t?[12] The answer is that evolution punishes "s...s" and rewards "cool guys". A man who has had casual sex can easily leave without any responsibility, while a woman can end up with pregnancy and all the problems that a single mother has in a modern society, let alone in the pre-modern times. Infanticide has been often attempt to avoid that problem. Of course, our intention isn't to judge promiscuous women, but to explain the reasons why traditional societies look at these problems the way they do.

Besides that, most men feel the urge for self-affirmation in sex that lasts relatively short period after a sexual act, or successful conquest, and therefore many men constantly search for new "flesh". Most men can't satisfy such lust for attractive girls because such girls are inaccessible and rare, so they're ready to compromise. Alpha male[13], a powerful man with high social position who can use above- average social resources, is in a position to choose among many, primarily physically attractive women. We have to say that according to women, the alpha male is a man with social and natural resources. Physical appearance isn't that important. With men, it's the other way around. To them, physical appearance is more important than the wealth or social status of a girl.

The girl we took as an example of an attractive lady doesn't have a small problem. Hegel believes that first she has to recognize herself in the person she's in love with in order to be self-acknowledged and receive recognition. The problem is because a

---

[12] It's not the level of this book to say fully the quoted noun here, which is still in everyday use.

[13] Today, the term *alpha man* is devalued, so men are divided into alphas and betas, while the author's opinion is that there are many shades of men, starting from alpha to omega and that full-blooded alpha men are extremely rare.

man, who has it all and analogous to her is in a position to self-acknowledge himself sexually with larger number of women, even though they may be attractive only on the surface, but that isn't generally a problem for a man. In order to avoid situations of constant humiliation caused by cheating, which such alpha males incline, an alpha female may be tempted to make a relationship with beta, gamma or even a delta man. Although she may be able to keep such a man under control, she won't receive love recognition because she won't be able to recognize her qualities and traits, or her social position in him.

The second option, which happens to alpha females, is to stay single, and in this way, they don't get love recognition either. The alpha woman is actually in an impossible position to get love recognition in the way that Hegel thinks it's possible. Still, the recognition of the audience remains and according to us, it isn't insignificant. Therefore, an alpha woman can be happily in love with a beta man too.

Since we've given explanations regarding the problems of unwanted pregnancy, we also have to take a look at the desired pregnancy. Besides socially acceptable forms of the desired pregnancy, in a community of a men and a women who meet moral and legal standards, many women who are trying to catch alpha males or other men on a social scale above the average woman, use the tactic "catch a hot guy by getting pregnant". We see that there are cases when unprotected sexual intercourses are acceptable to a woman. A real alpha man won't fall for such women's tricks. However, since society is weak concerning that matters, there's a pressure on alpha males including legal regulation, to take responsibility for such matters. All that corresponds to a type of a woman who's (driven by her primordial instincts to find a good provider) ready to do anything. We can't approve social values and legal norms that protect such female preferences. We live in an era that is too liberal towards women. In most countries of the Western civilization, women have the right to abortion without any rights of men in the sense of vetoing abortion, while on the other hand, if a woman decides to give birth, a man can't refuse to pay alimony in case he doesn't want to become a parent. Many civilizations that collapsed in the last stages of their existence have been liberal towards women's manipulation. In our opinion, there's a causal link between those phenomena, which we'll deal with in the second part of the book.

It's known that the ancient Greeks criticized Etruscans for being too namby-pamby towards their wives, and Etruria fell under the rule of much weaker Rome which wasn't that numerous at the beginning, but it was determined by masculine characteristics. Before that, we have an example of Sparta that has been collapsing with the rise of female power. Nowadays, we can mention the example of the US and the EU, which have increasingly less power in international relations, and that coincides with the growth of female power. Not to mention Serbia, which experienced the greatest humiliations and defeat in modern history at a time when it was led by the dictator – henpecked husband, who occasionally had to listen to his wife's orders, no matter how meaningless they were.

That issue is important, but we'll deal with it in the second part of the book, and now we'll get back to our topic. Here we must mention extremely masculine Conan's qualities. He has the opportunity to live a life full of joy with his sweetheart, but he decides to achieve his goal regardless of the wishes of his beloved one. The Barbarian even leaves his girlfriend so that she can't distract him in his life mission. The Cimmerian shows the qualities of a first-rate man regarding women. The Barbarian's will overcomes any urge that could turn him aside from his path, including the charms of his loved one.

Now, we'll deal with omega woman and omega man. Omega woman would be a girl of extremely unattractive appearance, while omega man would be someone who has minimal social power and minimal ability to spend resources. We're talking about people who can't count on the admiration of the audience. What's left to them in that case? For metaphysical and physical reasons, which we can't discuss now, most people are, if not on the margin, then below the average in terms of their abilities, income, looks, etc. According to our solution, inspired by Milius, they can get recognition by becoming the part of the audience. They make the audience and they decide who alpha male and alpha female are. Of course, that's the most achievable in liberal democracies. An average, in fact, a below average person is the one who buys the cheapest goods, rewarding certain industrialists or wholesalers in that way. The richest family in the richest and the most powerful country in the world is the owner of Walmart, a retail chain that has achieved success thanks to cheap goods. Countries, which produce the cheapest goods, have the largest economic growth. The most popular serials and reality shows are those that address the simplest audience and human urges. Since in the past the primary audience consisted of kings, dukes, courtiers and other aristocracy, actors couldn't be buried in cemeteries where normal people were buried. Actors were despised class. With the growth of the power of the ordinary audience, and the rise of the third class, actors have been becoming more and more popular, richer and they have had a higher social status. Nowadays, actors are politically influential too, so Arnold Schwarzenegger, who plays Conan the Barbarian, has become the governor of California. Ronald Reagan has achieved even greater success by becoming the president of the United States and the winner in the Cold War, and today even an aircraft carrier is named after him, according to United States ship naming conventions. There are many examples that confirm our thesis, inspired by film *Conan the Barbarian* - public recognition is crucial and decisive social recognition. Thus, we can solve Hegelian problems related to recognition. In that context, there's an interesting example of the Roman Emperor Nero. Although he had the political power as a tyrant whom no one could confront, and he sent many people to death without thinking, all his life he was longing to be sincerely acknowledged by the audience as a great and talented artist. Even in warring societies, heroes wish to be in an epic poem and get the recognition of the audience in that way.

In this chapter, we've been mostly dealing with the interpretation of Hegel's idea of recognition, which has been presented in *The Struggle for Recognition* by Axel Honneth, but we've also looked back on Kojève. It's important to make a distinction between Hobbes and Hegel's viewpoints of social conflicts. While according to Hobbes individuals fear for their lives when being attacked and their property taken away, Hegel argues that an individual has a feeling of being ignored by other social subjects. The assaulted individual doesn't react aggressively to the attack on his property only because he wishes to preserve it or because of mere vengeance, but because he wishes to be noticed by others. The destructive reaction of a party excluded in social interaction has a goal to draw attention. In the conflict of two sides there's the attention of both sides directed to each other - there's some kind of recognition. Personal legitimacy implies that a person requires recognition, i.e. recognition of his qualities, which leads that person to struggle to life or death. A person can come out of that fight with understanding himself as a person with some rights, because the subject ready to fight to death deserves a legal recognition. That happened in the English and French revolutions.

Lower class was ready to life or death fight and they gained legal recognition. Higher class has lost its exclusivity, although in the case of England not completely. It's interesting that Alexander Kojève believes that Hegel with his idea of fight to life or death has anticipated the way of thinking in existentialism. The point is that in existentialism the awareness of the possibility of individual freedom is conditioned by anticipation of the certainty of one's own death. That's particularly present at Heidegger and Sartre who are existentialists but at the same time atheists as well. Heidegger believes that life is nothing more than a movement towards death, and that ordinary people don't want to be aware of that. People live in a state of "being stuck" in their daily routines where they use their mind only as an instrument to solve everyday problems.

The process of thinking is moving from one to another everyday problem, not wanting to recall the necessity of death. An average personality settles into routine and customs established by social norms. On the other hand, an authentic person, aware of the inevitability of death, chooses a mission that will fulfill his life. That's how his freedom is manifested. Conan's project is his intention to punish Thulsa Doom. Because of his mission, he rejects the opportunity to enjoy love and warm home, which he could have made if he had followed his sweetheart's intentions. The Barbarian leaves her when she's tried to distract him from his life goal. Thus, he shows extremely masculine traits.

The following question may be interesting for us: If people are ready to fight to life or death for something immaterial, such as recognition, how do such genes survive in human race? Isn't it more rational to fight only for tangible resources that will enable survival and raising children? Does an irrational struggle for recognition have its evolutionary advantage? Let's assume, like we know from everyday experience, that not all people have such a strong desire to risk their lives for honor. Let's use simple math to help us. If people ready to die because of honor, exterminate each other, how do they leave their descendants? Why don't they die out over time? Especially young men are those who are willing to die for honor, which further reduces the possibility of leaving descendants, since they have high mortality rate at young age. Even if young men entered marriage and had children, their widows would be left without the support of their chosen ones and the survival of their children would be reduced. Is there a rational answer to those questions? The answer is actually very simple. Those who win and survive in the fight for recognition improve their social status. Although the mortality rate of those people in history has been very high, those who survive are able to impose their power on others. Aristocratic classes or castes were created by such people who survived the battle. The fact that the mortality rate of those people is high doesn't really matter, because when the winners get the power, they become more attractive to the opposite sex and therefore have the possibility to leave more descendants. One genetic study has shown that Genghis Khan, who's just that type of man according to our knowledge, has about twenty million direct descendants. One episode from that conqueror's life speaks a lot about what kind of a person he was. At a time when he was young and hadn't yet become powerful, warriors from the neighboring tribe took away his wife, In that part of the world, taking women away was something quite normal, and most people reacted by finding another woman, but not Temüjin. The future world conqueror was determined not to be treated that way. He organized warriors and made a war to get his wife back. It was one of the first successful war missions out of many, which he had launched.

We must present here an assumption about the origin of some of the most famous poems of Serbian epic poetry. Vuk Karadzic believed that Serbian epic poetry was very old and that it used to deal with some topics related to some ancient times. With the disaster on the Maritsa and Kosovo, the main topic becomes the loss of state independence and all the other distresses that accompany the nations that have lost their national sovereignty. Banovic Strahinja is a poem with the action set on the eve of the Kosovo battle, but we believe that it dates back from much older period and that it's adapted to current events. The plot and action correspond exactly to the historical case of Genghis Khan. Of course, we don't think that the poem has anything to do with the historical figure of Genghis Khan, but we do believe that it refers to some hero from the ancient Serbian past. Considering the ethnogenesis of the Serbian nation, the poem can have three sources: one is Slavic, before the arrival of the Slavs to the Balkans; the other may be related to the indigenous people of the Balkans who make the part of the genetic basin of the Serbian nation.[14] In

---

[14] In the period after the first edition of the book, more is known about this matter. According to male haplogroups, Serbs are about 55% of Slavic genetics with a relative majority of the specific branch of I2 haplogroup characteristic for the Slavs. About 10% belongs to I1

our opinion, it's most likely about the Serbs – whose name we bear - who as a warrior caste imposed on one group of the Slavs in the Ancient era. The dominant theme of the poem is the struggle for the recognition of the protagonist, who doesn't allow the others to treat him in that way. He's ready to fight for his reputation and the opinion he has about himself - that he's special. Unique Banovic Strahinja doesn't want to be like other men from society and period similar to the one in which Genghis Khan has grown up. While the others accept their fate, Strahinja fights for recognition of his personality, which mustn't be ignored. Only later in the Slavs agricultural-patriarchal process and the Christian vision of the indigenous population of the Balkans, the accent is transferred to tolerance of cheating.

In the warlike-nomadic world, named after the original Serbs[15], full of constant insecurity and abduction, the loyalty of the snatched woman, for whom an average man wouldn't even fight, isn't the most important issue. It's a pity that the old Serbian history has been neglected in Serbian science as if nothing existed before the Nemanjic dynasty. Serbian epic poem gives many possibilities for research. That's particularly the case with the poems with ancient motives. In *the Death of the Jugovic Mother*[16], the end is extremely pagan and it undoubtedly presents Jungian archetype of Mother Goddess.

In the end, we must conclude that irrational motives that make people gain recognition they think they deserve from the other members of society, even though it includes their readiness

---

haplogroups characteristic for Goths and Normans. The rest belongs to the people who settled in the Balkans before the Slavs. Genetics denounced the autochthonous thesis about the Slavs as indigenous people who inhabited the Balkans, and it's been abandoned in archeology and history a long time ago.

[15] Perhaps in the ethnogenesis of the Serbs a small war tribe close to the eastern branches of the Indo-Europeans played a certain role.

[16] A famous Serbian epic poem about a mother who found her nine sons dead, including her husband Jug Bogdan at the battlefield on Kosovo. Her pain grows and she dies at the end of the poem.

to lose their lives, are evolutionary very useful. Peace has an alternative. It's quite certain that Nietzsche would be pleased with that observation. The struggle for recognition doesn't have to be merely a matter of a warrior. Just as we've seen in the solution to our problem, the opinion of the audience or the public is crucial for recognition. Besides warriors, who believe that recognition of the audience isn't irrelevant - which can be noticed in the popularity of epic poetry in warlike-aristocratic societies – I mean which hero wouldn't like to be praised in poems - business people, artists, scientists and, of course, politicians can fight for recognition in less warlike societies.

It's important to mention two points that are important in that struggle. One is the importance of the recognition of the opposite sex. Hegel believes that a person, who hasn't experienced love recognition, must remain frustrated and can't be the part of the community in the proper way. Even an alpha male can't be alpha without the recognition of a woman. Every society sees alpha males differently. In warlike culture, it's the best warrior, in trading culture it's the most successful merchant. However, in every culture, a mandatory characteristic of an alpha male is that he must be wealthy. Even in communist regimes that insist on equality, and which have almost all failed or accepted undemocratic capitalism, such as China, women were trying to conquer men who had an impact on the distribution of social and material resources. On the other hand, civilizations that eroded the alpha male institution -as in the case of the Etruscans, who equated the power of women with men - collapsed. Generally, cultures that strive for equality are collapsing. The EU is the next candidate because it's trying to equalize different nations artificially, so the introduction of the same currency and similar interest rates has led to an economic crisis, let alone different mentalities. And that's the case with the peoples of related cultures belonging to the same civilization. It's clear that mass immigration of very different peoples in the EU can only aggravate things.

Another matter, which is important in the fight for recognition, is that you'll get recognition easier if you unite with someone in your fight. This is for purely practical reasons. Genghis Khan as well had to organize some people together to accomplish his goal. That's one way how people create the society of atoms. In the second part of the book we'll deal more with the origin and significance of the group in human evolution. People rarely confront each other one on one. The struggle for recognition is most often the struggle of social groups for recognition. We've mentioned the English and French revolutions, but we should keep in mind that most people belonging to a socially disadvantaged group have a greater chance to succeed if they're united. It's an important social glue that's incompatible with simple political atomism. The Roman proverb divide and rule[17] speaks in favor of it.

---

[17] from Latin dīvide et imperā

THE IDEA OF OVERMAN

Today we live in a period where primitive and egocentric hedonism is the main value of several generations. Precisely that hedonistic culture makes us weak in comparison to the cruel historical currents. In Serbia, that can be easily seen by the behavior of the political "elite" towards the citizens. Domestic politicians lead a policy based on satisfying the wishes of the present generation, at the expense of the future generations. They don't differ from the general world trend. The leaders want to satisfy the "herd", as Nietzsche would say, to hold the power as long as possible. Nietzsche's philosophy is essentially hedonistic, but opposed to satisfaction of superficial life pleasures, which can be understood from the following verses:

O man, take care!
What does the deep midnight declare?
"I was asleep -
From a deep dream I woke and swear:
The world is deep,
Deeper than day had been aware.
Deep is its woe -
Joy - deeper yet than agony:
Woe implores: Go!
But all joy wants eternity -
Wants deep, wants deep eternity."[18]

---

[18] **Zarathustra's Roundelay** is a poem that figures as a central motif in the book *Thus Spoke Zarathustra* by Friedrich Nietzche There are a number of different English translations. This one is from *Walter Kaufmann.* https://en.wikipedia.org/wiki/Zarathustra%27s_roundelay

At first sight it seems as if Nietzsche was aligned with the present period. But we can't take it lightly. Pleasure that Nietzsche appreciates is some higher pleasure. Ordinary satisfaction that ordinary people enjoy isn't valuable according to him. Epicureanism, utilitarianism, the types of hedonism that are based on pain avoidance and the calculation of average pleasure aren't worth enough. All types of pleasure that aren't related to strong will are for weak people.

Let's imagine a modern man living in an eudaimonic utilitarian culture whose aim is to live a happy life, avoid pain or satisfy consumer needs that are often artificially created. A man who can't resist satisfying his consumer preferences even at the cost of getting into constant debts and seeming bankruptcy[19] is a man of a weak will, a representative of the evil in the new morality of the "overman" who Nietzsche develops in his book *On the Genealogy of Morality*.

Take an example from not so far Serbian past. When the first big shopping mall (Novi Merkator) was opened in Belgrade in 2002, the mass of people who came to the opening couldn't even wait for the mall to open officially, but turned its uncontrolled consumer urges into glass breaking at the entrance to that building. By doing so, they showed that they are people of weak will who can't control themselves. According to Nietzsche, all that is a sign of life's decay. The situation isn't better in the rest of the world. The mentioned event is nothing compared to Black Friday in the United States. The Serbs had an excuse that it happened after the wars and sanctions, when they were hungry for everything. And indeed, although today there are big sales in Serbia including Black Friday, nothing similar to unrestrained predatory mass of people fighting for goods can be seen, as is the case in the United States.

---

[19] The truth is that debts and bankruptcy become more probable for most people, with longer period of validity of Fiat currency, that is, credit money.

Let's try to take a look at Serbia from Nietzsche's point of view in order to understand better his position, taking into account the knowledge and prejudices of our countrymen and contemporaries. Firstly, he opposes state. He doesn't believe that the state is national for the following reasons. The creators of the state aren't people but individuals. "Overmen", people of noble spirit, strong will, people with an artistic soul but selfish and ready for cruelty, warriors, heroes, noblemen but nobles turned to the future, not the past relying on their pedigrees, people who respect tradition, people who love life and pain, which is a part of life, people who want to rule over others, people who want to move up, people prone to higher pleasures, power- loving people, people who don't need another world to enjoy themselves, aristocrats, those who defend themselves, those who won't suffer, people with great passions, people who give, but not because they're merciful but wealthy, people who rejoice, individuals, those who constantly control themselves, those who can be thankful for a long time and those who are capable of getting revenge after a long time, grand, rich in character, rich in spirit, strict towards themselves and towards those who they consider equal, people above morality, advocates of war, advocates of freedom of death - suicide, courageous people, those whose enemies both fear them and hate them, those who are cleansed from plebeian, aesthetic people with sharpened senses, people who can, with their minds, encompass a multitude of connections and relationships at the same time such as Napoleon's mind and Christ's heart, or to put it in a nutshell - "overmen". The main objection to Nietzsche's description of "overman" is that he's reduced to a set of predicates. It's probably the best, instead trying to find in Serbian history people who fit that description.

At first glance, there are the founders of the modern Serbian state, Karadjordje and Milos. Karadjordje is a real tragic hero. The man, who Napoleon acknowledged to be a better warrior than himself, certainly fits into Nietzche's scheme. Besides that, Karadjordje killed his stepfather when his family was running away from the Turks. It was at the time before the Serbian revolution, when Karadjordje occasionally led the life of a hajduk[20], while he lived as a civilian in the meantime. His stepfather's spirit was broken and he wanted to surrender and expose the whole family to danger so that men lose their heads and women and children fall into slavery. Karadjordje didn't want to be betrayed by his stepfather so he raised his hand, i.e. a rifle, against him. We must bear in mind that at that time of patriarchal Serbia a stepfather had a status almost equal to a father, so in fact Karadjordje committed patricide. He also killed his brother Marinko based on rape accusations. Karadjordje was also the founder of the dynasty, or future nobility. He was a man of great soul, strong will and determination, he held onto his own and the dignity of the nation, a hajduk, a warrior, the hero of a tragic fate. A man who saw the ruin of his own enterprise, which had to go to exile and didn't lose faith in victory until the very end. Tragedy is Karadjordje's fate. He's a true example of a flesh and blood hero and a meritorious candidate for the title of an "overman".

The man who ordered his murder partly because he wanted power, and partly because of his interpretation of the national interest, Milos Obrenovic, Karadjordje's best man, was given the mandate to become the new Vozd[21] after more than a brave decision to stay in Serbia after the collapse of the First Serbian Uprising. He made that decision fully aware that he could easily end up on the spit. Milos Obrenovic is a ruler who fits into Machiavelli's assessment of what ruler should be like. Milos was brave as a lion and he showed it several times by risking his life both in war and in peace, and at the same time, he was cunning as a fox. He had to fight with the Turks both in Serbia and in Porte. He was continually suppressing the Turkish power and kept spreading the Serbian one. Everything he grabbed from the vizier's rights he took for himself. Sultan recognized him as the rightful Prince, and

---

[20] Hajduk is a type of a peasant irregular soldier who has a reputation of a bandit or freedom fighter.
[21] Leader

Milos became the founder of a dynasty. A man who used political killings to keep his power, a tyrant, a man of iron will and strong instincts, a passionate man. A rich man, who helped art and people who live from culture. In short, an "overman", according to almost all Nietzsche's predicates. While Karadjordje is more Napoleonic type of an "overman", Milos is more Borgian type. However, those two historical figures don't fit fully into Nietzsche's definition of an "overman". Both of them were illiterate, while Nietzsche's "overman" is an educated barbarian. Karadjordje is too moral for Nietzsche's taste, while Milos Obrenovic showed weakness when he felt guilty after the murder of the political father of the Serbian modern nation.

In that historical event, Milos has fit into the pattern of the rebellion against the father of the community, which Freud has explained in one of his most important works *The Uneasiness in Civilization*. Freud tried to explain the occurrence of religious rituals, religiosity in general, and their relationship with morality. He connected it with the rebellion against the father of a social community leader in prehistory. Sons, winners after committing patricide feel guilty and remorse so they develop religious rituals trying to relieve their psychological tension in that way. Over time, the memory of that event takes the form of a myth. In ancient Greek mythology, that event took the form of a myth of Cronus (time), who castrated his own father Uranus (heaven), so that he wouldn't have more sons with whom he would share power. Cronus was eating his children not to have anyone who would overthrow him, but his wife Rea managed to deceive him and save three sons: Zeus, Poseidon and Hades who managed to oust him from power. In that version of the myth, despite the violence, the father is "only" castrated (Uranus) or expelled (Cronus). Freud believes that there is a memory of that event in Christianity because Christ takes upon himself the sin that society committed against the father creator in the past by its rebellion. Contrary to the biblical tradition, the father of psychoanalysis believes that at first there was a deed, then an act of rebellion, and followed the word, which would try to justify and atone for that deed. Similarly, Milos Obrenovic committed the political patricide, and then he repented and built the church to show his repentance.

Those are examples of two men, although the term man isn't adequate for them anymore, since they fit into Nietzsche's profile of an "overman" according to almost all their qualities. Also, there's an example of two Serbs who fit into that profile in our epoch. The first one is an educated man in the field of social sciences, the creator of a party and state entity, a politician who managed to survive an economic blockade by his own people, a poet, a man charged with war crimes, a very witty person in hiding under the false identity of an alternative medicine specialist - of course, it's Dr. Radovan Karadzic. The other one is his political associate and opponent, a general, a man of strong will, a warrior, according to many people a hero, and according to others a criminal, a man who experienced a family tragedy, but it didn't distract him in carrying out his leadership duties, but made him even stronger. Both of them are Dionysian types. There is a gentility of a higher type of a man in the fact that they've opposed many Western countries and succeeded in gaining something for the Serbs. Only people with strong personalities are able to make such ventures. They didn't care which force they were facing, but how significant was what they were defending. Also, they have the feature of respect of tradition.

Karadzic is a person who kept the spirit in his life even as a fugitive. According to his nephew, he visited Venice and Italian championship football matches. It's interesting that the crime attributed to them raises an interesting question regarding Nietzsche's understanding of morality. Since the base of Nietzsche's understanding of virtue is the determination where strong will is good and poor will is bad, we can't judge these "people" based on that. The fact that they're accused for murder doesn't make them bad according to Nietzsche. Don't kill! - a Christian command that makes life difficult for people forced to defend according to Nietzsche is a nonsense. Doesn't life consist of murders? The criminal label attached to Karadzic and Mladic's[22] personality, according to Nietzsche, doesn't diminish their approach to the idea of "overmen" at all. "Overman" is a being above morality, used to killing. When we take into account that there's revenge behind those crimes, from past times, it only makes them even closer to the ideal of "overman". According to Nietzsche, the utmost virtues of an "overman" are enjoyment, love of power and selfishness, and if one needs to kill someone in order to get power, then it isn't something to be condemned.

Although to us, the people of the 21st century living in the age of human rights domination, some things that've been said so far, don't seem to fit into the definition of the word "overman" , according to Nietzsche that could be interpreted as our flaw - we're too indoctrinated by Christianity and humanism which he doesn't appreciate. All those Christian virtues such as compassion towards other people are only an expression of weakness and plebeian morality.

According to his philosophy, Christianity opposes life because it rejects current sensual world over some above sensual world. Ideologically, Christianity deals with the poor, the unhappy, the sick, those who are thirsty for justice; in short, Christianity is a consolation for all the losers of this world. That's what Nietzsche disapproves. He believes that such values have ruled Europe and limited great men, since Christianity has been the dominant religion and ideology starting from the Milan edict until his (Nietzsche's) period (the end of the 19th century).

---

[22] I have to point out that there was no serious evidence against Karadzic and Mladic for the crimes they were accused of. It's interesting the West feels the need to judge its enemies and present itself morally superior. If the West had been so morally superior, it would have had a balanced approach to all warring parties and their interests at the very beginning and there wouldn't have been fratricidal war at all. I say fratricidal because Muslims in BiH, like many Croats, are obviously of Serbian origin. Today genetics as well show autosomal similarity in the area of the Shtokavian dialect. But the constant quarrel of small nations suits to the elites of the West.

Another quality makes Karadzic and Mladic Nietzsche's "overmen". It's the artistic, mythical and irrational understanding of the world. According to Nietzsche, truth is something that doesn't really exist, art is more truthful than science or a rational attempt to understand the world. Karadzic is dinaric[23] type of a man. The characteristic of people from Dinaric Alps is their desire to be recognized.[24] Karadzic grew up in the world of epic poems. Much of Serbian epic poetry is related to people's frustration because of the loss of state independence and first getting into vassals position, and then, the situation's been getting worse with every following century and it's ended up in almost slavery position. We can see that this frustration's been a source of poetic creation since after the liberation of Serbian countries that type of poems disappeared, while we could experience its great comeback during the fight of Bosnian Serbs for their independence and statehood. It's hard for the Serbian poet and myth maker to stand the reality. The reality under the conqueror, who is - to make it worse - of different religion, is even more difficult to explain when we take into account the religious moment. By definition, God is good, and again he allowed Christians to fall into slavery! How to explain it? The creator of Kosovo myth uses a typical Christian explanation of the other world. Prince Lazar and Kosovo heroes sacrificed for the sake of justice and the other world, which is better than this one, even though they had the opportunity to win the victory on the Earth. "The earthly kingdom is small and the heavenly one is forever." Such a Christian explanation Nietzsche despises. There'll be more about that in the chapter on the antichrist. There's another element by Serbian poet which is pagan, male and which doesn't admit defeat. In his poems, he praises hajduks and uskoks[25] – people who don't want a life of slavery. Not only did they want to live like serfs, but many of them

---

[23] A mountain on the border of todays Bosnia and Herzegovina and Croatia- Dinara. Dinaric alps are mountain range in Balkan.

[24] Jovan Cvijic's human-geographical research.

[25] Irregular soldiers who fought against Ottoman empire

didn't consider the possibility of becoming ordinary citizens when it came to military duties of Military Frontier. The dangerous life of a military frontier soldier, who besides military duty has freedom to feudals, is certainly an interesting life circumstance. Nietzsche would surely like such qualities, praised in epic poetry.

The most popular character in Serbian epic poetry is a barbaric aristocrat, who has almost all the features of Nietzsche's "overman". A nobleman, accordingly educated, but also restless dionysian tyrant who shows his power with every following adventure. He doesn't refrain from hitting and robbing a woman who insults him.

"God aid thee, dear sister!
Is blood-brother Philip within?"
But Philip's wife made answer:
"Get thee hence, starveling dervish,
Philip is no brother to such as thee!"
When Prince Marko heard that
He smote her in the face with the palm of his hand.
Now a golden ring was on his hand.
And it did scathe upon her visage.
And put out three sound teeth from their place.
Then he took from her three rows of ducats
And cast them into his silken pocket."[26]

This rascal, besides beating women, warring, robbing, cheating and drinking, possesses traits that make him even too ethically developed for Nietzsche's "overman". That's most evident in the multi-platinum hit of epic poetry where after the victory over the great hero won by cheating, epic superstar cried:

"God of Mercy," quoth he, "woe is mine!
For I have slain better than myself."

---

[26]

https://archive.org/stream/balladsofmarkokr00lowduoft/balladsofmarkokr00lowduoft_djvu.txt

Definately too much for Nietzsche.

We'll attack here, the national myth, the supranational myth, the myth of a classless society, the myth of liberal democracy, the myth of a multicultural society, the myth of private property, the myth of higher race, the myth of the moral organization of the world and the possibilities of morality itself and some other myths, proving that Nietzsche's desire for power has a logical-ontological basis, which Nietzsche hasn't developed in a satisfactory way because of his methodological determinations. For example, why aren't morality and life compatible categories? We particularly have in mind Christian and humanist morality.

Let's make an example where we'll show that a moral choice in relation to life extension is impossible and we'll make the first step in proving the incompatibility of morality and life. Let's imagine two survivors of a shipwreck in a lifeboat located in an area where there's no possibility to be found. Besides that, they know that they haven't managed to contact anyone and sent a call for help while the ship has been sinking. Everything has happened at lightning speed. They're both aware of their situation and that the tide'll take them to the shore within two weeks. The problem is following: They have very little water and, under the most favorable circumstances, the chance to survive is maximum a week. Survivors of a shipwreck have the opportunity to survive only if they get rid of another shipwreck survivor. Provided they both want to survive, the only real option is to get rid of the other one, which is - to kill him. So in that case life and morality logically exclude each other. Also, there's another possibility - that one of them commits a suicide because he doesn't want to survive in that way. However, in that way as well, morality and life must logically exclude each other again. He, as a moral person, can't survive. The same case is when both of them are ready to risk life by playing Russian roulette, believing that the case will determine who'll survive. Life and morality exclude each other in that case too. They have again succumbed to suicide, becoming suicides. According to Christian morality, that's also unacceptable by most other ethical theories. Kant, who has a highly developed ethical theory, rejects suicide. It's paradoxical that Nietzsche, who permits suicide because he doesn't care about morality, allows the possibility of the seemingly most right solution - that the case decides who'll survive. However, like we've noticed, the point is that life for both of them at the same time is impossible and that the classical morality has no solution to that problem until it allows suicide to be a legitimate moral act.[27] Nevertheless, there still remains a problem of the incompatibility of morality and life in that case. The biggest problem is that we don't have a serious reason for moral objection to shipwreckers if they both want to live. Where's immorality if they're both trying to kill each other? Or if one chooses to kill another? Is there morality if there isn't life which would apply it?

Let's apply that case to the world in general. We have a reason to believe that cyclical economic i.e. energy crises necessarily repeat. Being hungry is also an energy crisis. In order to function, a person must eat. In doing so, many people, in order to satisfy the perpetual energy needs of their bodies, eat animal food. They kill creatures who feel emotions and who are aware of the world to some extent, in order to satisfy the needs of their stomachs. Even vegetarians demand the killing of living things to

---

[27] Such cases with shipwreck survivors often happened in the past centuries. The law of the sea - unwritten code that sailors from Europe were applying, said that in such situations, lot drawing would decide who would be killed so that the other can drink his blood and eat his flesh and survive in that way. At the end of the 19th century, three British sailors, who survived a shipwreck, were convicted of murder because they applied that code by killing the fourth sailor. Although the public was on their side, under the pressure of intellectuals of the Victorian era, they were convicted of murder. Since that case, that code wasn't officially applied. The development of technology and rescue services contributed to reduction in the number of those situations after the Second World War.

feed themselves. However, we can assume that some people can survive eating fruit and berries that fall off trees. Does that make them moral and are ordinary vegetarians and meat – eaters immoral?[28] I don't know the answer to that question. Perhaps there'll be delicious synthetic food in future so the issue will be obsolete. But that's not the point. We might be struck by severe droughts and all food resources might be used up. Even for the production of synthetic food, we need energy and other resources. What if energy crisis starts that'll prevent the production of any food? There's a real possibility for that, and according to the knowledge from the history of mankind it's practically certain. After all, the big bang itself could have been the solution to the energy crisis of the previously existing universe. The example involving famine can be formulated to be logically consistent, but we'll use artistic means. While I was reading the book by Nikola Milosevic "Literature and Metaphysics", it reminded me of the novel "The Golden Fleece" by great Serbian writer Borislav Pekic, who describes the famine that arose in the tempestuous period of Serbian history. I'll quote the part from Miloševic's book where he comments and values that part of Pekic's description:

"Pekic's method of dispersing illusions is portrayed always with some fine, ironic distance towards matters being dispersed. The same hint of a gentle humor that's already familiar to us hovers above the apocalyptic scene of the destruction of the Njegovan family's goods.

However, we have to point out that Pekic's humor has a cosmopolitan force. Cosmopolitan, since it runs deep under all the illusions and deceptions, finding only that of "human, too human" there.

Perhaps for such artistic viewpoint on the world, which is free from any narrow-mindedness and self- delusion, is the most

---

[28] We should stress here that people don't become vegetarians only to save animals. Many Indians are vegetarian for religious reasons, and some people become vegetarians because of health. Adolf Hitler was a vegetarian because he was prescribed a wrong diet.

characteristic one author's commentary from the second volume, dedicated to the motive of cannibalism, which escalated at the end of the 17th century due to great famine. If the boy Simeonoulo was a bit more mature at the period described in the novel, according to the author: " in Belgrade, at the times of the Great Migration, he would find the strongest evidence for that traditional suspiciousness of people, who have been making the mental basis of the Simeon's trade with them for centuries. He would find that human layer that distinguishes him from beasts was thinner than the breath on the mirror and that we have to keep breathing on to the surface of the mirror if we want to preserve it."

And immediately after that gloomy judgment about the alleged human nature, we find in Pekić's novel the following tragic report about what was happening at the time of famine.

"The breath on the mirror disappeared," the writer said. "Misery helped with famine, illness, fear and death wiped out the last trace of human glow ejected from our animal skin by thousands of years of oppression. The natural heirs of the Byzantine Empire, the descendants of the almighty epic singing heroes were eating each other in the ruins, in streets, in the yards of churches. The healthy ones were sneaking behind the weak, expecting them to die and to prolong the lives of the healthy ones in that way. The strong were chasing the weak in the dusk. The mad ones didn't care about anything. They were already there – on the other side of the Big River."

Those words could only be written by an artist who was fundamentally free from illusions, an artist who resolutely ended with mythic awareness in all its forms."[29]

Our goal as well is to terminate with mythic awareness in the forms we've listed above. National, supranational, classless, multiclass and the other types of society must collapse when left without energy, when the famine rules. Pekic writes about the Serbs who eat each other in order to survive. The same would

---

[29] Nikola Milošević, *Literature and Metaphysics*, Official Gazette of Serbia and Montenegro, 2003, p. 257

happen to any nation or group of individuals in such a situation. In the times of crisis, people are ready to kill and eat each other. What we want to say in defense of Nietzsche's immorality is that people as specie aren't evil because they wish to be evil, but because nature created them so. Not only did it make them like that, but they can't be different if they want to live. In such cases, situations without any resources, morality is unaffordable to those wanting to survive. Morality is a possibility only for those willing to give up on their lives. They don't have to kill themselves, it's enough to behave morally and they'll go down. Nature, the world, the cosmos doesn't reward morality, in Christian and humanistic terms, but the opposite. Morality is possible only in quiet periods of human existence, when there's no hunger, wars, economic crisis, and even then most people can't afford it. Morality is the greatest luxury and only wealthy and dignified people can behave according to its norms. By the very fact that morality is possible only in peaceful periods, it loses its meaning. Is a good man the one who is good only when everything in his life goes well? Certainly not, but if he's good in the circumstances we've stated, he'll not be able to survive and transfer his genes, so good people will die out. Good people can exist only in rich societies, and even then in small numbers, since the first crisis will exterminate them. Self-delusion is shown in most people thinking they're good, but circumstances always give them a chance to realize their misconception. The morality that can exist in the real world is limited, first to time and place where there is no catastrophic resource scarcity, and then to a group of people who's your ally in crisis. Thus, total nationalism is practically impossible, because within a nation there are natural conflicts of interest that prevent the permanent preservation of the alliance called nation. In catastrophic crises, private interests become much more dominant than national interests. Nationalism has a chance in another way. In the case of Karadzic - he lives in a period when the national myth possesses vitality and rational justification. Although in the long run no nation can preserve common interests - thus the history is full of people who have disappeared or blended to other, new nations (let me remind you of the case of the British and the Americans, whose economic interests were in contradiction, despite the common origin), there are periods of history when a nation can be homogenized. Threat by a common enemy is often a factor that makes people join in alliances called nations. The 1990s made the myth of nation real. The Serbs fought for real resources with others. Serbian people in Croatia and Kosovo have lost their living space and material resources. Many of them lost their private properties, and without that, even according to some classical liberal philosophers such as Locke, there's no life. What has destroyed the myth of nation in the 1990s as a long-lasting ally are people who have managed to profit from the calamity of their own people. The fact that war profiteers have left the war without any legal consequences strengthens our belief that the nation is a myth. The selfishness of majority further strengthens our opinion. Most Serbs aren't ready to expose themselves to troubles because of the Serbs expelled from the Republic of Krajina and from Kosovo. Selfishness is stronger than the national spirit. Selfishness imposed by evolution. Tested recipe for survival.

I believe we've said enough about the myth called nation, and that myth is the most real. Now we'll deal with the myth of supranational. That myth's more unreal, more light and can be more easily refuted than a myth of national. Supranational state-like structures with the exception of the EU were created by war, where one group of people gained dominance over the other. Egypt, China, Persia, the Macedonian Empire, Carthage, Rome, the Russian Empire, the Ottoman Empire, the Spanish Empire, the Austro-Hungarian Empire, the British Empire, NATO; they're all the creations of war victories. Force, interest and inertia kept them together. As soon as the force that kept them together weakened, they started falling apart. China is a special case. The small states that existed on the territory of today's China were early in history (the 3rd century BC) under one authority. For a long time, China didn't have any competition, until the time of the developed

European colonialism. China lost wars only against Mongolian barbarians who wanted to rule rather than destroy the Chinese state. The goal of Mongolian aristocracy and other conquerors was to preserve the Chinese state as a source of resources. China wasn't a competitor, but a prey – a mass subordinated to few people. It's Nietzsche's supranationalism. A group of masters ruling over the herd. There isn't any universal morality, there's only an aristocratic morality and there's a morally of the defeated, dominated servants and slaves. People aren't one class.

There's no need to waste words on India. There's a caste system, which shows that people obviously don't have morality equal for all. We can't use the word morality unambiguously, in terms of universal morality that doesn't include interest and which is the same for all people. We can talk about morality that regulates relationships among people taking into account some common interest of a specific group of people. Even that morality has a limited effect because, as we have seen, it must be suspended in disastrous situations. We'll notice that the supranational creations were falling apart to national components during their collapses, which shows that the national myth and national morality - here we take those words in a non-universal meaning – are something more permanent and more real. When we say *national,* we imply more ethnic than political meaning of that word.

Some empires are conquered by force of the others, so it's clear that in such cases, morality doesn't play any role in building supranational creations. Persia was defeated by Macedonia, Cartagena by Rome, the Ottoman Empire was partly defeated by foreign powers, but mostly by Russia, and partly it was disintegrated into its ethnic components. The Balkan nations have risen from the ashes, the ethnic Turks have formed the Turkish political nation; the Arabs tried to win their independence, but new masters - the English and the French imposed on them.

In the case of the Roman Empire, it's clear that it was created by a well-organized military force. The beginning of the ruin of Rome corresponds to the impossibility of its expansion. There were poor, but violent barbarians in the north of Europe. The war against them was expensive and unprofitable. In the south, they conquered everything they could; only the desert remained. There was the Atlantic Ocean on the west to the Roman Empire; the East was interesting for the expansion, but the successor of Persia - Parthian Empire got on their way. Due to its inability to absorb the new territories to *"feed"* itself, the Roman Empire was dying a bit by bit by consuming its substance, until its corpse served as energy for barbaric vultures, mostly of German origin.

There's no need to go further since we can notice that empires are created by feeding on new territories and their resources, and when they are no longer able to do that, when an equally powerful enemy crosses their way, they begin to collapse by eating themselves up. Supranational creations also must destroy each other in order to survive. Natural laws are such that there can't be supranational creations of "good" people.

We must especially look back at the European attempt to avoid new wars. The problem is the following. European most developed countries have become dominant in the world due to the European way of education, the scientific method, the capitalist economy, and the mutual warfare competition that has stimulated innovations. In Max Weber's work, we can see the importance of a rationally organized state for the development of modern capitalism. England's been a leader in it and it's become the world dominion, despite the fact that at the beginning Spain and Portugal have had a large number of colonies. In their expansion, the European forces have faced competition consisted of feudal empires burdened by religious education and societies, which were at the level of hunter-gatherer communities. None of those two types of societies could compete with critically thinking European education and capitalism, which is very rational when it comes to the exploitation of natural resources. Today, the situation is completely different. Formerly backward feudal empires such as China and vast forests with hunter-gatherers natives such as Brazil have taken over the European mode of education and the capitalist economy. Due to their cheap labor, those and some other countries have become such a big competition to old European states and their direct successor, the United States, that the old capitalist countries have plunged into an economic crisis. The West has to choose – either to collapse slowly and lose its position, or to try to regain the old state of things with the help of its current military superiority. So, the matter is reduced to the dilemma of the shipwrecker, and the one who wants to survive, in fact , live well, is forced to take immoral actions. Although, of course, the real enemy of the people, which we can place under the political meaning of the word West, is their ruling elites that are increasingly opposing the interests of their nations.

The situation isn't different with working class either. The working class of China and Third World suits the fact that a factory in the West is closed and moved to Third World. Workers, although belonging to the same class, are confronted with the shipwreckers' dilemma. One's loss equals other's gain. Just look at the example of Zastava Vehicles, a company from Kragujevac. Fiat, in order to remain competitive, has to move its production to countries with cheaper labor. That's good for the workers from Kragujevac in case the production moves to Kragujevac, but that'll mean job losses for Italian workers who'll remain without income. In this case, we can see that the working class can't be united because it has conflicting interests.

The problem isn't the capitalist way of production, as some Marxists may suggest. Even in the conditions of central economy planning, there are decisions made to do harm to one group of people and to bring prosperity to others. A decision on where some goods will be produced in the socialist economy will also create workplaces in one place at the expense of some other place. If the distribution of resources is such that those who's got the job and those who hasn't got it, recieve the same benefits equally, then the injustice is done against those who work.

Natural laws break all the myths we've listed, there's only one reality that's in line with Nietzsche's philosophy. Only the will to power is lifelike, the one who wants to survive or live well, must make immoral choices from the classic morality point of view.

Since this book's titled *the Philosophy of Conan the Barbarian*, we must also look back at this work of art. Conan the Barbarian found himself in a situation similar to our shipwreckers. He's been thrown in an arena to fight to life or death. In fact, he's been pushed into it, without understanding the world of that battlefield, nor its purpose. Being attacked by an experienced fighter, he defends himself. Instinct teaches him how to act, and killing an opponent is the only thing he can do to survive. There's a similar scene in *Spartacus* by Stanley Kubrick. Spartacus, starred by Kirk Douglas, loses a fight in the arena against a black slave gladiator. The black slave decides not to kill Spartacus, although that's what's expected from him, and he's trying to kill the rich Romans in the audience instead. The black gladiator dies without carrying out his plan. He acts in the way that we have the feeling that he's acted morally. That action's basically suicidal because he had no chance to survive with such decision. The Barbarian's position is different. Conan must survive in order to carry out his life plan. That's why he can't afford himself a luxury to act morally like the black slave's acted. Thus, the Barbarian's similar to us, real blood and flesh people, who have to make moral compromises from time to time and suffer various humiliations in life, hoping that we'll carry out our personal life plans.

Milius's scene where Conan is thrown into arena is a metaphor of an old philosophical observation. Being thrown into the real world is the understanding of the stoic philosophy, which has developed in the late ancient period when the institution of polis was minor and when man more than ever before, saw himself as a walnut shell floating in the ocean. The World Empire - Rome, made an ordinary man feel like a grain blown all over by the winds of history. That supranational creation has contributed to the acceptance of determinism in the lives of ordinary people. A man is thrown into the world without any instructions to help him save himself from the position of a walnut shell floating in the ocean. The philosophical solution of the stoics is that reasonable people accept the determination of the outside world by developing freedom within their souls. Suffering and readiness to any caprice of fate is a distinguishing feature of a stoic. That philosophy's become popular throughout the Roman Empire. Both slaves and upper classes accepted it. Even the Roman Emperor Marcus Aurelius became a stoic. Conan the Barbarian as well accepts his fate while fighting in arena - the phase of his life, which we mentioned. Life or death - it doesn't matter to him. Still, because of his life plan and the inability to make a moral choice, he accepts, according to Nietzsche, the only healthy life possibility – the fight. Despite the philosophical peace chosen by ratio, life instincts intensify and the Barbarian begins to enjoy killing, success and recognition by the audience. The Cimmerian is successful, and Nietzsche's philosophy is a philosophy of successful people.

THE TRIUMPH OF THE WILL

The title of this chapter is borrowed from the film by Leni Riefenstahl, where she uses artistic means to promote the national-socialist party in Germany in the 1930s. Our goal in this chapter is to study the link between the Nazi[30] movement and Nietzsche's philosophy. There's no doubt that there's a connection, but how much Nietzsche's really responsible for Nazism is arguable. There are many explanations for the Nazi movement's success, and we'll look back at the possibility of the recurrence of such organizations. The largest competitors of Nazism are liberal democracy that's been a worldwide trend since the 1990s and Marxism that's been declining in all parts of the world, with exception of the US campuses.

In order to understand Nazism, we must understand the intrinsic problems of liberal democracies with capitalist economy. The problem of liberalism (liberalism in the sense of classical liberalism, or what the United States calls conservatism), which we'll deal with here, is the solitude of an individual in the enemy world. While in the Middle Ages, a man was a member of a wider family, some class, or some craftsmen's association during his whole life, in a liberal period, a person can be a member of a private company as long as the company benefits from him. In the market economy, a man is a commodity and has his use and market value. If he's young, healthy and with decent education, he can live a beautiful life. As soon as his health weakens and he gets old, and some new technology relativizes his professional qualifications or makes him superfluous in that field, a man becomes an outsider in such a world. Liberalism can't restrict the market economy. The characteristic of liberal democracies is their tendency towards the rational arguments concerning the society

---

[30] We'll use that popular shortened term for National-Socialism.

organization and the use of resources. The main problem of the market economy is exactly the rationality we've mentioned. Rationality of doing business inevitably leads to such technological development, which aims to expel man from production process. It isn't just about replacing workers in production, but also in service sector. There's been an obvious tendency towards that ever since the Industrial Revolution.

While the largest number of people once worked in food production, today agricultural production in developed countries is highly automated and it doesn't require a great number of people. Since the period of the Industrial Revolution, new job openings occur in those sectors where technology's still incapable of replacing humans.

Another factor in new job openings is the needs of people who were lucky in the market economy and have money to spend. It can't be predicted which sectors will have new job openings and that gives an additional sense of insecurity to employees. An ordinary employee is in between the fear of being sacked and uncertainty about finding a new job. The uncertainty in the capitalist way of doing business raises important questions. We'll start with this one: Is there progress?

At first glance, that question seems pointless if we take into account technical innovations and the progress of medicine that enables people to live longer and be healthier. However, that question is aiming at something else. Is there any progress in terms of social relationships and human emotions? Will there always be landlords and peasants? In liberal societies, private property institutions and market relations dominating among individuals make one group of people more successful, richer, and able to hire those less successful, making them dependent on them. Although the authority changed its form in comparison to the period of feudal system, the content's remained the same. There hasn't been much progress regarding social relations. To be honest, we should admit that social mobility's theoretically advanced in liberal societies. According to theory, everyone can succeed and become "a landlord".

Blue blood castes, where it's almost impossible to enter, don't exist in liberal society. In practice, however, most people repeat the success of their parents. The starting position is most often crucial because the success of your parents can provide resources for your own development and personal competitiveness. However, there are people who create something even though they originated from low social class with a bad starting position. That can trick us in our assessment of progress. Even in the Middle Ages, there were people able to achieve more than their parents. Frequent wars were opportunities for ambitious people's advancements. Mrnjavcevic, Hrebeljanovic and Brankovic are noble families created by people who have exceeded the initial positions of their parents. Someone can say that it was extremely difficult to achieve such success in becoming a nobleman. We can answer to that with a question: Is it easy to become a multimillionaire today?

It would be too much to say that there's no progress in relation to the Middle Ages, especially when we remember the cruelty that people were expressing towards each other at that period. Yet, there's no essential progress, since the reasons that enable humanity in the modern age come from greater social wealth. People are good in favorable circumstances. If a cataclysm that would impoverish the entire society had happened, people might have become even crueler than they used to be in the Middle Ages.

It remains to be answered whether there's progress concerning human emotions, in fact whether people are happier than they used to be. It can't be denied that people easily get accustomed to good. On the other hand, it's very difficult for them to get used to bad. That feature comes naturally for the human race and certainly for other rational and evolutively successful beings as well since it supports survival. That feature itself prevents progress in the field of emotions. People can't be ever satisfied.

Another important factor doesn't support the idea of progress. There always must be some scarcity for rational beings to use their resources effectively. If there wasn't shortage of goods, ratio wouldn't be needed for survival. To be stupid or intelligent – it wouldn't matter, since the result would be the same. If God (meaning the demiurge), under the assumption of creation, had been still active in the process of man's creation, he would have been forced to give scarcity to the humankind from time to time, or ratio wouldn't develop. The same case would have happened in a somewhat different scenario - if he had created the universe so that natural laws make the world create rational beings. Scarcity is necessary for the development of ratio.

Uncertainty is the emotion that's been present by rational people in all periods, and it'll always be present, provided they feel like living. In hunter-gatherer primitive society, man was in uncertainty because of dangerous animals, the exhaustion of hunting ground and conflicts with other tribes resulting from exhausted hunting grounds.

In agricultural societies, human being feels insecure due to climate conditions, the occurrence of pests or barbarians. In market societies, man feels uncertain because of the possible market collapses, transportation accidents, spoilage of goods, pirates and other robbers. The industrial era brought the uncertainty in relation to workplace, which is needed to afford food, clothing, housing, education of children and the greatest pollution in history. Each of the mentioned societies and the ways of obtaining goods brings uncertainty and discomfort. The philosophy of existentialism, a relatively new wave in philosophy, has dealt with that feeling of discomfort. That's a bit surprising given the presence of worry, fear, uncertainty, anxiety and similar human problems since the beginnings of human rational thinking. It seems that the reason for the development of that philosophical approach is people's abandonment of various mythical forms of thinking.

The insurmountable problem of liberal societies is that the rationality, which is their main characteristic, introduces the natural selection. Thus, society loses its protective role. Nature and its cruel laws where only the strongest, the luckiest and the most capable survive, are presented in market economies. Society doesn't have its own identity, society is nature.

So far, we've been dealing with the main competitor to National-Socialism, which seems to be a historical winner. Now we'll deal with another, in many ways similar attempt to overcome the world. The similarity between National-Socialism and Marxism, or Communism (socialism is step from capitalism to communism according to Marxism), is reflected in irrationality which they both contain.

Another similarity is that each of them singles out one class of people as privileged. In Nazism, master race is privileged; in that particular case, those are the German descendants of the Aryan race, tall, blonde, white people. In Marxism, working class i. e. proletariat, people without capital and property rights over the means of production is privileged. They both have the right to rule and, for certain mythical reasons, that's what they ought to do. Marx's basic thesis in his criticism of liberalism is the following: In a civic, liberal society, only one class of people gained freedom. Those were the bourgeoisie, who declared decisively for universal freedom during the French Revolution. Before the French Revolution, the nobility had certain rights greater than the other people, i.e. the Third Estate. The Second Estate, also protected, was clergy. By the Declaration of the Rights of Man and of the Citizen, all people have become legally and ideologically equal.

As Marx has noticed, in reality, there's one class of people who doesn't own any property and therefore can't have freedom either. While the bourgeoisie own the means of production, and with those means enter competitive market, the class without property can only enter the market with their own skin. Production and social relations are developing where the bourgeoisie exploit hired labor. During Marx's era, capitalism was really cruel: workers had minimal rights and worked hard for bare life.

In modern liberal societies, there's some protection of the working class, including all employees, from cleaner to engineer. However, in new conditions of global capitalism, there are small chances for that protection to withstand the competition of societies like China, India and other third world countries.[31]

Marxists believe that those relations will change with time and that the world will move from capitalism to Communism with the help of revolution. Communism is a state where private property is abolished: all large corporations and banks' capital is under state control, and those with no property have the power, and they abolish class system. According to that understanding of the world, the transition from capitalism to Communism is in relation with historical necessities. For some time, Marx considered necessary for all societies to become capitalist first. Later, he changed his mind by encouraging the Russian communists trying to move directly from Feudalism to Communism.

That myth has many similarities with Christianity. The target group in both cases is the same - people who weren't present on the day when God was giving out luck. Both religions are eschatological, which means that they include in their beliefs a moment in the future that'll mark the end of the earlier history and the beginning of the golden era. In the case of Christians, that'll happen by God's will, and in the case of Marxists by the historical necessity - due to the contradiction of capitalism, a favorable moment for the revolution will come. Marxists will have to do some effort themselves.

---

[31] This book Serbian edition was written in 2010 and published in 2011. The appearance of Trump and other leaders, voted by those who want to protect their nation and their standard of living from globalism, show that modern democracy gives a chance to those ready to fight.

It's incredible how people are ready to believe in fairy tales. Uncritical consciousness must have been useful in evolution. That's not unusual if we know that the ratio has the bad trait of not supporting the will. Take war, for example. In the case of war between the opponents who are at the similar technological level, losses must be significant on both sides. Let's be reasonable, the probability that an ordinary warrior will survive a severe war isn't high. We'll illustrate that with the fact that 75% of German submariners lost their lives in World War II. That means that the ordinary member of that army branch had three times greater chances to die than to survive. If we also take into account the date of joining military, the probability to survive is even less for those who joined army earlier. Someone who joined the war in 1939 could hardly see the end of the war without any injury.

There was a similar situation with the Anglo-American bombers crews. Those who enlisted into army earlier were reducing their chances of survival with every new mission. But imagine those warriors giving up due to reasonable fear for their lives. War couldn't have been won, and the other party relying on mythical consciousness would win the war. The world where the Axis Powers won the war wouldn't be a good place for survival of the defeated. You can get the picture about that in Philip K. Dick novel *The Man in the High Castle*, which deals with the world where the allies lost the war. Therefore, calculation isn't of some benefit to the specie.

In every war, there're survivors. Besides that, if the survivors had relied solely on their reason, and realized that their chances to survive had been extremely small, as we've already mentioned, perhaps they would have given up fighting, and as losers, they would have had less chance to bring forth their offspring. The winners or survivors were those who had such mind that was telling them that despite the small chances of survival, they themselves would still survive. They were able to create a myth of their particularity, some kind of connection with the cosmic order and providence. They believed they were somehow more important, or luckier than other people, or that they had a lucky charm that'll bring them success. Such mythical consciousness hasn't only been useful in war survival, but also in large exploration missions as well as commercial ventures. If people had had in mind that fact which showed them how small possibility to achieve their goals was, they wouldn't have achieved a lot as a race. Specie composed of cowards can't expect success. As a reminder, it's enough for few men to achieve success in order to extend the species. Things are different with women, so it's logical that women are usually more conservative and less inclined to embark on adventures.

We'll notice that men in order to achieve success must be grouped together. In that way they increase their strength and chances of success in the battle with nature or other men. Individuals who would try to resist the group on their own, wouldn't have chances to succeed. In order to survive, men have to unite. War is nothing but the fight of one group of men against the other group. As we've already noted, rational thinking doesn't always help; it's natural that there's a need for a myth that'll make a certain group of men special and in that way strengthen their faith in victory. Defeated group of men particularly need such myths. We'll cite a recent religion as an example. It's Rastafarianism.

The Rastafarian movement developed in the 1930s and apart from the decade when it was formed, which coincides with the decade when the Nazis came to power, it has more similarities with National-Socialism. The movement developed in Jamaica, a former English colony inhabited by descendants of black slaves. Except that they were legally released from slavery, the lives of black people haven't improved much. Even today, Jamaica is a society where the effects of slavery are felt. For a black man, true equality has remained a dream until this day. The Rastafarian religion was created under the influence of the prophecy of Marcus Garvey, who told his followers to look to Africa where the Black King would be crowned when he was leaving to the United

States. The crowning of Ras Tafari, that is Haile Selassie, and the fact that his titles were matching the statements from the Book of Revelation, inspired three men: Leonard Howell, Joseph Hibbert and Archibald Dunkley to believe that the Emperor is the God. The new Rastafarian religion is based on six beliefs: 1) Haile Selassie is the living God. 2) A black man is the reincarnation of Israel. 3) A white man is inferior to a black man. 4) Jamaica is hell; Ethiopia is paradise. 5) Haile Selassie arranged for Negroes to return to Ethiopia - their old homeland. 6) A black man will rule the world in the future. There're two specific features of that movement - the unique hairstyle of its followers, which resembles a lion's mane and the religious use of Indian cannabis (hashish, marijuana, weed), in Jamaica known as "ganja".

From the above said, it can be seen that, like German Nazis i.e. members of the people defeated in the World War, had the need to build an ideology that would make them special and better than other races and nations, the same need had the defeated and subordinated members of black race in Jamaica. Those Jamaican black racists claim and believe that a white man is inferior to a black man. On the contrary, the Nazis, German white racists, believe in the opposite - that a white man is superior to other races. The Nazis specifically marked the Jews - the nation / religion of non-European origin, which has been part of German society, as inferior and they were successfully exterminating them throughout Europe. They also believed that their historical mission was to rule the world and, according to them, other lower races e.g. the Slavs too. We can be surprised that the Rastafarians aren't suppressed by the government in democratic countries. It's probably because of the general ignorance of the teachings of that movement and the lack of belief in their power.

As stated above, we can see that Nazi ideas aren't something that's typical only of German culture or white race. Hatred towards other groups of people is universal regardless of skin color, nation, or religion. Surely that such hatred had been useful in evolution, otherwise it wouldn't have existed. It's difficult to accept it, but it's true that those who hate others and are ready to exterminate them and take away their living space are rewarded. The Jews themselves, who've been the victims of Nazi persecution, have committed genocide in their history against the Canaanites, the original inhabitants of today's Israel. The Jews exterminated those people and took away their land on the pretext that it was God's will. After all, the Jewish religion itself fits our profile of group myth. The Jews are the chosen people and they have a special status with God.

Marxism also fits that profile, but aims at the supranational class of people. Those poor people of all classes have the right to take from the rich, but not only from the rich, to satisfy "justice" and fulfill historical need. That teaching's evolutionarily useful for the following reasons. Women generally tend to win over men who are in better social positions. That evolutionary strategy provides greater chances for their survival and their children development. Marxism is a teaching that justifies attempts of men from lower social classes to gain social resources, giving them even the right to kill other men who are already in good positions in society. The history of the Second World War in Serbia and Partisan leaders taking the positions after the war show the purpose of ideologies such as Marxism in the real world. It's a justification for taking from the rich among their own people.

In this book, we're dealing with various myths busting, and it's an opportunity to devote to the myth of the national liberation struggle. The results of that fight against the Germans are very modest. The contribution of the partisans to the victory over Nazism is insignificant when compared with the main figures of the Second World War, such as the US, the USSR and the UK, while the number of victims is very large. For example, the Syrmian Front was broken with heavy casualties when the Red Army was already in Berlin. Yugoslavia was practically "liberated" by the Red Army. It expelled the occupier. The modest contribution to the Second World War of Tito's partisans, with large casualties, and especially large and unnecessary civilian casualties, is disproportionate to how much that great struggle contributed to improving the social status of the communist elite. Tito was the God on the Earth, he had what he wanted, and his officials and comrades mostly lived in joy and happiness for the rest of their lives. We can see how that fight for resources (at the time of occupation and among their own people) was successful from the very fact that those whose property was taken after the World War II, haven't still gained the right to return it, even though the alleged democrats[32] gained power. Those democrats are of partisan origin and they still have the tendency to satisfy their own needs at the expense of large, at that time economic sacrifices of their own people.

In every society there's a significant number of men who aren't sufficiently sexually competitive due to their low social status. The defeated and subordinated within an already structured society also need supranational ideologies with that target group. Just as Nazism is trying to justify the race and ethnicity struggle and crime, ideologies like Marxism give justification for class crimes. From the moral point of view, Marxism, which doesn't have its own ethics, is unable to solve the problem where all ethical theories fail, and that's scarcity of basic resources, which happens periodically and necessarily to people. We presented that problem in the form of a ship wreckers' dilemma. What if Soviets found themselves in a famine situation due to central economic planning and there were resources only for the survival of the half of the population? Such disasters aren't unusual for the Marxist economy. Let's recall the constant scarcity in the USSR and famine in Ukraine during Stalin, or in China in the sixties when it took millions of lives. In today's North Korea, famine is a permanent state of affairs.

How to act if there's only enough food for half of the population until the next harvest? If the communists act according to their main principle of equality in the distribution of goods, all people will die and there will no longer be people with the highest

---

[32] In 2019, restitution is still ongoing.

morals. On the other hand, if they act immorally and contrary to their ideology and separate a part of the population who'll die of hunger, they show that Marxism doesn't have solution for the shipwreckers' dilemma.

Marxist competitor - Nazism has other issues. Nazism is trying to provide a better position for a group of people of common origin, which includes people of different social strata. They make promises to all of them that they'll be the part of the ruling caste. The problem of Nazism is that all people are of common origin, and even genetics has proved it. Moreover, the Europeans are quite similar to each other. According to autosomal DNA of the Europeans, who are divided into various nations and states, they're more related than people in India according to their autosomal DNA, although India is a state and has long been a cultural and civilization entity. German pure race genes can't be pure when shared with other people, especially with the Europeans. Among the Germans, the relative majority of men originate from the Bronze Age conquerors that were coming over period from steppes of today's Russia and Ukraine. The relative majority of Danish male population has haplogroup originating from the prehistoric hunters - gatherers. The blonde hair gene appeared in prehistoric times northwest of the Black Sea, in Ukraine or in Lithuania, and it relatively quickly spread across Europe due to sexual selection. Thus, blonde hair isn't of Nordic origin, as being suggested by Nazi ideology. Male German and Slavs ancestors came to Europe almost from the same place, below the Urals. Historical Aryans may not have been blonde, although they are genetically related to the European peoples. In fact, according to genetic research, haplogroup R1a1 is the most prominent among the Slavs of European people and it is found in high percentages in South Asian people in Aryan influenced territories, which leads to the thesis on the common origin of the Aryans and the Slavs, while the Germans have the most common haplogroup R1b, which is the most widespread in Western Europe. As it can be seen from the latest scientific results, Nazi racial theories had a romantic background. But we mustn't be naive, Nazism and Marxism don't need science and morality as products of reason. Reasonable arguments aren't sufficient to hold theory in those cases.

A reasonable man is very naive if he's trying to take that approach in resistance to those ideologies. A Nazi or a Marxist is just a man on the surface following some argumentation. Their true motives remain hidden from themselves. The main motive of those people is the reproduction of their genes, and morality or science has nothing to do with it; they're just an impediment.

Having said all the above, we can reflect on the point of Nietzsche's philosophy so that we understand it in a simple way. Although we can sometimes interpret that Nietzsche believed the Nordic type of man to be superior, the idea of the ruling race, which is the main idea of Nazism, isn't the core of Nietzsche's philosophy. Nietzsche thought that all beings desire power, and that it appears disguised even in those who don't want to admit it, like Christians. Nature is such that there'll always be those who'll rule and those who will be ruled by. Rulers have their own noble, warlike, aristocratic morality that fits those who rule.

On the other hand, those who are subordinated develop their own morality of the oppressed, which differs from aristocratic morality by its purpose and content. That morality explains the world through the concepts of sin and reward; it promises the other world because in this one, the oppressed are dissatisfied. Nietzsche disapproves the fact that Christianity's been the ruling ideology for so long, although it's the religion of the oppressed. He's found that such situation isn't natural. He has similar opinion about socialism and liberal democracies. According to him, the value of plebeians, mass, "herd" as he calls them, mustn't be universal value.

Race isn't the most important for him. He values India for the caste system where it's known where everybody belongs, although Brahmins and Kshatriyas there, i.e. the ruling class of priests and warriors doesn't consist of blond, blue-eyed white men. Although the truth is that those people are Aryans but they aren't of Nordic origin. Nietzsche celebrates the ruling class, not the race, which got its position by fighting. If by any chance the Balkan criminals enslaved the Nordic countries and became the ruling class, while the Scandinavians became the ruled "herd", Nietzsche would be on the side of those successful inhabitants of the Balkans.[33] Nietzsche, unlike the Nazi, wasn't anti-Semitic and didn't have high opinion of the Jews haters. Christians, socialists, and liberals he disliked more. All those who accepted slave morality. Slaves don't have life instincts strong enough to fill them with desire to be recognized, so they deny the existence of the powerful by resenting them. Bad master's qualities are those, which fill them with fear, and good ones are those that enable them to survive: loyalty, modesty, obedience, patience, mutual help and service, loving their close ones. The qualities of independence, power, love of power, which are the traits of masters, are believed to be evil. There's also a problem of free will, created by slaves. Thus, they created self-denial that it's possible to be someone else, although the bird of prey can only be a bird of prey, no matter how much the lamb wanted it to become a lamb.

According to that philosopher, the state was formed by a group of aristocratic warriors who enslaved some peaceful but numerous population, and imposed their will and laws on it. It's similar to what Conan's historical Cimmerians have done with the Thracians, or the Bulgarians, in the same area, but later with the Slavs, the Normans with the Saxons, the Arabs with the Egyptians ... According to that theory, state has nothing to do with the social contract. Those aggressors, commanders, and masters don't need contract.

The state, i.e. the civilization, ruled by war elite that came to power contrary to social contract, is also portrayed in *Conan the Barbarian*. The very name of the ruler, before whom Conan and his

---

[33] Now, a better example would be migrants from Africa and the Middle East.

company were brought, says how much he respected contracts in his struggle for power. The name of this King is Osric the Usurper. He's portrayed as once mighty Northerner, whose strength has left him. The King, portrayed by Max von Sydow, isn't able to confront Thulsa Doom, a charismatic demigod who has seduced his daughter. King Osric the Usurper asks the Cimmerian and his company to return his daughter in exchange for great treasure. Thus, Conan gets an extra motive to fight Thulsa Doom.

Apart from the struggle for recognition, which is the Barbarian's motive in his fight against Doom, there's of course revenge, and the type of revenge that Nietzsche appreciates. However, besides those motives, there should be strong will to accompany all that. When we named this chapter after the name of Leni Riefenstahl's film, we had in mind the part of the film where Conan, unlike other enslaved children, continues to turn the wheel persistently, defying his unfortunate fate. That will, which is able to withstand the icy bites of blizzard and vampire bites of sunlight, draining the water from Conan's body, building its body, its weapons for the fight with Thulsa Doom, in spite of everything. *Will* is a term that plays an important role in German philosophy. Kant has been the first philosopher of will, and according to him, will is the most important in the struggle of being with himself to do moral duties. "Blind will" has played a special role in the teachings of Schopenhauer. Nietzsche named his unfinished work *The Will to Power.*

What's bad in Nietzsche's philosophy is his determinism and his denial of free will. By doing so, he underrates any success. If everything's determined and there's no free will, then Conan isn't meritorious for being in a terrible place, and diminishing the horror of such place by enlarging his body. Nietzsche's aristocrats don't differ essentially from slaves or stones. They have no responsibilities, no merits, and they can thank pure luck to be the ruling class. Having intention to get rid of morality by abolishing free will, Nietzsche has abolished the reasons for admiring an "overman" or any great man in general. His idea of self-overcoming becomes meaningless due to determinism. Self-overcoming includes a personal decision and the struggle of will with its own urges that prevent us from realizing our own intention. That difficult struggle, which can involve physical pain and spiritual distress, becomes unrecognized. We can feel the pain and it may seem to us that we're overcoming it through suffering, but we won't be meritorious for that, we'll become ordinary puppets.

The only way out for Nietzsche is to get rid of determinism, which would greatly undermine his philosophy. However, without it, the qualities he admires have no value. "Aristocratic morality", under the condition of free will, is admired by those who accept it. That morality's the only one which can endure logically the trial of shipwreck survivor's dilemma. Killing the other person for resources isn't immoral. In the world of war, that's completely normal since the war exists thanks to the struggle for resources. The fight of tribes, nations and empires against each other is basically a fight for resources.

Since nature is such that it promotes that type of behavior, every attempt to avoid such a struggle must seem naive to us if we want to be those who survive. We'll quote the part from *Nietzsche and the Nazis,* a book by Gyoergy Lukacs, where he showed that kind of naivety: "The great post-war task of democracies is to discover and ideologically eradicate that tendency" (it refers to the tendency of broad layers of educated classes towards a fascist "point of view".) because only the extermination of those roots can destroy the fascist ideology and prevent its renaissance in the future. I'll allow myself to illustrate that ideological situation with a small example from my experience. In the second half of the war, I held lectures to German senior officers. Most of them were captured near Stalingrad. During the lecture, we had long intimate discussions. Almost without any exception, they were all convinced that Hitlerism would collapse sooner or later. They were all rejecting the teachings of Hitler and Rosenberg. However, most of them didn't change their point of view regarding the essential issues and in terms of aggressive imperialist ideology, there was almost no change. They rejected Hitler and Rosenberg and returned to the philosophy of Nietzsche and Spengler. From that belief, they wanted to wait for the outbreak of the third and, hopefully, more efficient world war.

That's the danger, and that's our problem. Today it's not a big deal to reject Hitler and Rosenberg. Anyone returning to Nietzsche or Schopenhauer, Spengler or Klages (of course, they could be Ortega and Gasset as well) could begin moving in the direction of a new fascist ideology, which might no longer be called fascism, and which may deny Hitler and Mussolini, but in essence, in inhumanity, in renouncing progress, democracy and reason, it may be even worse. "[34] Lukacs isn't only naïve, but a real hypocrite as well. Senior German officers are much more honest than him. Lukacs doesn't mention red Soviet imperialism that led to the war with Finland and taking part of its territory, the annexation of the Baltic States, the division of Poland between Stalin and Hitler. That part was written in 1946 after Stalin's occupation of Eastern Europe. All that was the expansion of the Soviet empire, the manifestation of power, or has Lukacs thought that it's been progress and democratization of the conquered territories?

One must be unfair not to recognize that type of imperialism opposed by American democratic imperialism. Just like our theoretical addition to Nietzsche predicts. For Nietzsche, the essence of all is irrational will to power, and according to our expansion of Nietzsche's theory there's a rational reason of the struggle for resources. Having the will to power means desiring resources in order to increase the possibilities to survive and a quality way of life. Democracies are equally hypocritical in their appeal to human values and progress. Are democracies ready to give up energy needed to run their economies for the sake of humanity? Historical experience has shown that they aren't. Even after the collapse of the Soviet competitor, the United States have

---

[34] *Nietzsche and the Nazis*, Gyoergy Lukacs, Culture, Belgrade, 1956, p. 13.

continued the struggle for domination and the desire to bring under their influence the countries rich with oil, the basic energy resource of modern civilization. It's hard for most people to accept the world of Nietzsche and Darwin, but that world doesn't ask if you're ready to accept it, it imposes its rules, and if you don't accept it, you'll be beaten and eaten.

THE LAND OF HIPPIES AND BEING OF NIRVANA

What motive drives the followers of Thulsa Doom? What's striking about their behavior? Let's look at those people when Conan the Barbarian meets them while looking for the way to the mountain where Thulsa Doom is stationed. The scene when he meets them is set in a landscape covered with colorful flowers. That should imply the role Milius has given them in his work of art and whom they should present. It's not hard to notice that they're in ripped clothes, skinny, that they've neglected their physical appearance, decorated themselves with flowers and singing. In them, we recognize people defeated by the world, people not ready to fight. They're looking for a way out of there, and that's what Doom promises to them. Milius portrays hippies BC.

The modern hippie movement developed in the United States, in San Francisco precisely, during the Vietnam War. The hippie movement insisted on rejecting the values of the American society. By values, they meant material values, the ethics of work, every aspect of fight and war. Hippies were often children from wealthy families who were financing their non-working way of life as long as they could. Those young people also rejected racial divisions that were much more present in American society in that period than nowadays. Besides that, they advocated free love, which meant casual sex without obligations. However, it seems that the most important was to avoid any kind of responsibility and *pain*.

That avoidance of pain resembles the ancient epicurean philosophy. Although today Epicureanism is known in a popular culture for its hedonism and insisting on a life filled with satisfaction, much of the Epicurean theory and practice is based on pain avoidance. It's a philosophy that gives a different answer to the same question in relation to the philosophy of stoicism. Like the Stoics, the Epicureans have tried to give instructions for life in an atomized supranational empire where old social connections and man's involvement in a community have disappeared. A man was exposed to some unpredictable caprices of destiny, and all that he had to bear alone. In Greek polis and tribal democracies, an ordinary person could have the impression that he influenced the decisions concerning his life. In the Roman Empire AD, an ordinary person really didn't have any influence.

Spoiled young people from mostly urban families could have some similar feeling. It's common that people living in abundance which they haven't earned by themselves, begin to develop some strange ideas about the world. They begin to think that it's possible to live eternally without responsibility, work and fight for survival. Thus, young people of the United States from the stated period don't differ from the young people from the ancient times who couldn't accept responsibility for their lives, and in their desire for someone else to think and work for them, they flee into an imaginary reality, becoming the prey of various obscure movements and sects. While yearning for a life without suffering, it's natural to avoid war. The real reason for American hippies insisting on peace is based on their fear of going to war. Why would anyone risk dying in some filthy war on the other side of the planet because of some vague goals of that same war, while a deserter could enjoy irresponsible life in the richest country of the world with a lot of even more irresponsible sex? Why would someone want to work to get something he already has without work?

The world itself gives the answer to that question. When you're without any income, you have to fight to earn it or you'll die, unless you want to completely abandon your dignity and live from begging. The same goes in case of war. People join in some warlike formations and in developed societies, they form armies to gain resources that will enable them to live, i.e. to have the dominant way of life. After all, the Huns, who have become the bugbear of ancient Europe, appear in history as a company of some poor people who were looting to meet basic needs. Having become skillful warriors, they seized power over European barbaric tribes and threatened Rome itself. The humble and difficult life that they were accustomed to, became an advantage that led to power. Contrary to that, the parents of civilized children, trying to give them everything, work to their own disadvantage. Those children, who aren't accustomed to work, war, sacrifices, become weak people and subjects to easier manipulation. In his work, *Conan the Barbarian*, Milius through artistic forms shows his scorn for such young people. As a chronicler of Conan's adventures, he speaks in a scornful, almost mocking tone and language about their messages to the Cimmerian. "They told him to throw down his sword and return to the earth. Hah! Time enough for the earth in the grave!" Of course, they are shown offering flowers to the Cimmerian as real peace "fighters".

After that scene with ancient hippies, as a contrast, Conan comes across a war shrine. To add a flavor of ancient times, Milius portrays it as made of menhirs, tall upright stones erected all over Western Europe. Some archeological sites from the Neolithic period are made of it, and even today, we aren't sure what their purpose was. The most famous are Stonehenge in England and Carnac in France. Conan's megalithic site also has a large altar. The megalithic stone formation is partly decorated with remains of warriors in armor with their weapons. With that detail, Million leaves you with your imagination. In the real world where a constant scarcity rules, their open graves would have been robbed for sure. Metal in the Iron Age, even before and after that time, has been too valuable to rest undisturbed on the unprotected warriors' graves. So many robbed Egyptian tombs testify that it's been hard to stay safe from robbers. Neither the secret barriers and mechanisms, nor a curse and human superstition have protected pharaohs from thieves. Instead of dead knights, Conan would encounter bare skeletons, and maybe not even those due to animal predators.

We mustn't forget that art is better than reality and that Milius has the right not to stick to realism in an effort to convey the mystery of this place. The chronicler intensifies the monumental impressions of the megalithic tomb with his comments: "Once upon a time some great people lived here - the Giants, the Gods - once, but a long time ago. " That is the place where Conan and the Wizard, his future chronicler, met. This encounter is a witty example of an attempt to present ourselves as powerful as possible in front of some unknown person. The Wizard and the Cimmerian end their verbal contest laughing, as two experienced and in some way truly powerful men.

Such verbal contests are already typical of children and they are very rational. Instead of wasting our strength on proving power, every time we meet somebody new, we will try to demonstrate power in a more relaxed way. The very physique of two individuals can determine the winner. However, the verbal demonstration can reverse this situation. We can mention some powerful and influential people or some well-known person like our cousin or a friend.

Later, during the meeting of the Cimmerian with his future chronicler, the wizard adds the historical weight to the sanctuary. Tumuli have existed since the Age of Titans, and great kings were buried there. The Wizard states an interesting feature of this site - that the fire does not stay on there. That is why he has to live in the vicinity. This man resembles the guardians of military graveyards, such as Zeitenlik[35], but in Milius's vision, he is also a priest. He sings to them about battles, heroes, witches and women. About all those, which collide with hippies' believes, excluding women, but ... I wonder: "What kind of woman loves a man of a weak will?" Hence, she herself must be a loser, who hers

---

[35] Zeitenlik is the largest military cemetery in Greece. It contains 20 000 graves of the soldiers who died in the Word War I. The largest part of the complex is Serbian Military Graveyard.

innate affection, that a woman has toward young children, conveys to the one to whom such affection can only hurt.

In the rest of the movie, Conan makes a naive attempt to infiltrate the ranks of Thulsa's followers, but they discover him. It's interesting the way the artist portrays these people. Pilgrims are camping near the mountain where Thulsa Doom is stationed. With Conan's walk through their camp, we get a chance to meet them. Based on the clothing they wear and the animals they use, they resemble the people of the Middle East, the part of the world where the first urban civilizations developed, affording opportunities for younger generations to grow up in the circumstances suitable for the attempt to escape the pain of this world.

Some of them are inhaling hallucinogenic vapors, others are singing gathered in a circle, a group of girls are using the name of Thulsa Doom for meditation. In their performance, they're pronouncing the word *doom* to concentrate, but there's no doubt that Millius is making an allusion to Om (Aum), which in Sanskrit literally means - yes or let it be. It's a Vedic syllable, which is chanted as mantra and the one chanting it brings the revival of supreme form of prayer to Brahman. (a prayer that brings power to the Vedic priests in the ritual of offering a sacrifice) In fact, Brahman is an amorphous sacred power that gives immortality even to Gods. That word is an unchangeable form of creative power taken by Brahman. Thus, by using that word we gain power. That's probably another Milius's mockery of hippies and their fascination with Indian and other Oriental teachings. In using the syllable Om (fiat!), there's nothing more but a hidden will to power, which can be asked from Gods, in fact the desire to be equal to Gods. Behind the hippie movement and their orientation to "being", "self" and other nonmaterial values, lies the disguised will to power. Hippies don't want to work and fight but to live and have sexual intercourses. They want something better and therefore they're looking for a way that'll make them powerful to do that and independent of that world of suffering. It's natural that they're attracted to religions similar to Buddhism, which we'll deal with more in the next chapter.

Besides that, we can see in the pilgrims' camp the people who're trying to overpower their bodies, but not in the way that the Barbarian adjusted his body to his personal goals, but by denying the spirit's need of body. That's another kind of retreat before the world where the body is seen as a burden. Resist eating, drinking, moving, getting all feelings numb to avoid exposure to the world, its demands and the pain it brings with it.

There are also those who're praying, seeking salvation, those who resemble Christians. Christianity is essentially a religion related to Buddhism because it's dissatisfied with this world (which we can't condemn), and also it addresses the target group of sufferers. Hippies, both those modern, and those ancient ones – Milius's share common features with the early Christians. Do not kill! Turn your left cheek if someone slaps you on the right etc... Honestly, many things related to Christ have been probably misunderstood. That call to turn your left cheek is pursuing dignity. In ancient times, the contemporary period of Christ's life, a person would slap on the left cheek someone who he thought to be equal to him as a challenge. Women and slaves were slapped on the right cheek, since 85 % of people are right-handed. Post Christian teachings have transformed that into an ideology of endurance without repaying evil with evil.

When Thulsa Doom's priests and priestesses appear, those miserable and wretched pilgrims turn to them, raising their hands and waiting for salvation. They remind of people to whom Nietzsche's Zarathustra is holding a sermon criticizing *the last men*, the type of small minded people who value comfort and equality above all; who are warm, who live their pitiful comfortable lives, who say : "We have invented happiness" while blinking. There are no rich or poor among them and they seem as if they stepped out of John Lennon's song *Imagine*. Zarathustra talks about those *last men* who he considers worthless to the crowd, who he considers chaotic enough to give birth to stars, people for whom he hopes that they can become "overmen" are, but they stop him with exclamations: "Make us into these last men!" That's what Milus's pilgrims look like and shout in themselves - Save us Doom, make us into these last men.

They're reaching out their hands to get white pilgrims clothes wishing to secure their place in Heaven. As if getting into Heaven is that easy. They believe that some simple prayer and service to some religious leader will bring them to the greatest reward. But even if it's like that indeed, and if they succeed in achieving their goal, they can also be disappointed, because Heaven can be misery – the doctrine of a great philosopher whose teachings we'll be dealing with in this chapter.

Already in the words of homosexual priest who addresses to Conan, Schopenhauer's philosophy, related to the Brahman, Buddhist and early Christian teachings, can be recognized – "How do you expect to reach emptiness without knowing your body?"

In order to understand better Schopenhauer's philosophy, let's begin with the following statement of this philosopher – "The world is my representation." Schopenhauer believes that this starting point of his philosophy is the starting point of any true philosophy. A person unaccustomed to the rigor of evidence in philosophy can take that attitude as unacceptable. We are used to consider rationally the existence of a tangible material outside world. So, let's deal with a problem in a philosophical way. Is there a sound, if there's no one to hear it? Is the table hard even if nobody's touching it? Are there colors that no one can see or, for example, if there were only beings, who see the world in black and white, would colors ever exist?

Schopenhauer has believed that we can't understand the world in no other way but through our sensations. We would have never known light if we hadn't seen it and we wouldn't have known scents if we hadn't smelled them. The world is originally known only as the content of perception and consciousness. It takes deep thinking to realize that light can be seen only by someone and noise be heard by the other one etc.. That's the assertion of idealistic philosophy which is contrary to naive, rational, realistic acceptance of the world by philosophically uninformed people. Although realism has a difficult task to prove the existence of an outside world beyond our perception, and no philosopher has succeeded in it so far, idealism has its problems as well. Thus, Schopenhauer can't tell the absolute criterion of the difference between a dream and reality, and according to him, there's no absolute difference. We can say that reality is a dream and vice versa. According to realistic point of view, a dream differs from reality in real images that aren't created on the basis of real objects, while in reality there are material objects behind images. The problem is that this can't be proved. We perceive both reality and dream through our presentations or sensual perception. The world of representation is a deception, a veil, a dream. We can't claim that behind those perceptions is some solid, real world.

According to Schopenhauer, the objects of our consciousness are real as such, as representations, that is their empirical reality. They exist as creations of a subject, on their own, without any reality, images as they appear to an observer.

The question of the outside world has another, deeper meaning: is this world only my representation? Is it, which I'm aware of only in a certain way, as well as I'm aware of my body in two ways (as a representation and as a will) on the one hand a will and on the other representation? Asking that question takes us from the world of presentation and introduces us into the world of will, takes us out of sleep and brings us into reality, takes us from the world of phenomena and introduces us into the world of *things in itself*. Kant has used that term *thing in itself* and it refers to the world beyond our power of perception and other kinds of knowledge.

If we were pure observational subjects, pure subjects of knowledge, then we would be given only the world of the presentation and we wouldn't be only the dreamers, but also dreamed of in a dream. But we are subjects, personalities, individuals. We perceive the world through a direct object – our body. This individual body has been given to us in two different ways. One way is a presentation in intellectual perception, as an object that doesn't differ essentially from other objects, and in a qualitatively different way, familiar to all of us and called - will. Every expression of our will is inevitably the motion of our body as well. Schopenhauer doesn't see expressions of will and body motions interrelated as causality but as heterogonous states. Will is given to us directly, and body motions as intellectual perceptions. Schopenhauer doesn't count willing decisions concerning the future in expressions of free will, since those are only the conclusions of the reason about what is desired in future. Every physical action is an objective act of willingness and vice versa, every impression on the body is at the same time an impression on the will, if that impression opposes the will - we perceive it as pain, if it suits will - we perceive it as pleasure. Therefore, pain and pleasure aren't presentations, nor can they be deduced from them. They are the direct affections of the will in its appearance, the body. They're forced instant desire or aversion of that impression that a body receives. According to Schopenhauer, the identity of will with physical activity is called the philosophical truth.

Other basic questions of philosophy are related to that fundamental truth, with an emphasis on the theory of knowledge and metaphysics. Those are issues associated with the existence of the outside world. Do the other perceptions of the observer (cognate subject) corresponds in itself something that's no longer a representation, something realistic, as our body's perception corresponds its will as a real basis? If the body's perception is the only one among the representations that has such a real substratum of the will, is there only one real individuum in the world? Schopenhauer is in danger of moving to solipsism here. That's a theoretical point of view where, in the absence of evidence of the existence of the outside world, I believe that it's certain that only I exist. That position of theoretical egoism is very strong and it's perhaps impossible to abandon it only with rational argumentation. Like many before him, Schopenhauer acknowledges insurmountable problems in mastering that view, but he continues to build on his philosophy.

Schopenhauer believes that the other representations besides those of our bodies corresponds something realistic. That reality is nothing else but will. Thus, in Schopenhauer's philosophy, the will takes over the role of *thing in itself*, will is a real reality unlike the representation. The essence of what constitutes will can't be defined by words, but each of us has the experience of will that's the aspiration for something. At least, that's how we feel it. Schopenhauer further reduces force, which is the basic phenomenon of the most developed science, i.e. physics, to will. In that way, he has reduced something unknown, inaccessible to something familiar to everyone.

Schopenhauer believes that the will is the essence of all nature. He thinks that the will can exist quite well as some unconscious force too. Schopenhauer finds that will acts blindly through animal instincts, thus proving that there can be unconscious will. By the term unconscious, he implies that it's without representation, and he also believes that our bodily activities such as digestion, breathing, blood running through our veins are unconscious manifestations of will. Conscious will is guided by motives, both of humans and animals; unconscious organic will of instinct and vegetability is guided by impulses, while physics deals with blind inorganic will guided by causes.

When we see an unstoppable rush of water running towards the depths, the persistence by which a magnet always turns to the North Pole, when we directly feel the load, whose tendency to the earth mass bends our body - then we won't need much imagination to get to know our own being, which led by the light of knowledge, strives to reach its goals while it aspires blindly and consistently to those listed above. In both cases, this core of every object in the world must bear the name - *will*. That reality, called will, makes the inner connection of causes and consequences. Inorganic world, flora and fauna, and finally — a man, are only different degrees of objectification or manifestation of will. It's the inner being of the world. The problem lies in the fact that the world that is the objectification of a single will can't have an aim, the will is desire in its core, pure desire and nothing more. It's a limitless, mindless, aimless aspiration. That aimlessness of the world's essence is objectified by the impossibility of satisfying the aspirations of any type of will. The inability to satisfy any aspirations is the basis of the eudemonistic assessment of the world given by Schopenhauer.

This philosopher believes that the struggle of natural forces for the gain of substance is intrinsic to nature and every aspiration in nature, every force is prevented by others in its full objectification. Schopenhauer has in mind that will is objectified in special identities that are in conflict with each other. For example, the will of a being that wants to eat isn't aligned with the will of a being that doesn't want to be eaten. Every objective will come across the resistance of others in an effort to objectify fully itself. Preventing the will that arises from the obstacles of those opposed to that will is suffering, and the attainment of the goal is called satisfaction. While endurance and suffering are unconscious, the will doesn't feel it. Conscious will feels endurance as pain, and satisfaction as pleasure. Since struggle is important to will, endurance is the main ingredient of will, and when taken into consideration that each satisfaction of one's need is negative, and when bearing in mind that pain raises with knowledge, then it's obvious that life is basically pain and suffering. Logically, it's enough to take into account Schopenhauer's assertion that the essence of the world is a limitless, mindless and aimless aspiration, to understand that for the conscious will, the world has to be a priori miserable. Should we satisfy all the aspirations, viewed in a global context, we would destroy the will that's the basis of the world, so there wouldn't be world at all. If there were no movements caused by blind desire, there wouldn't be any inorganic or physiological processes. According to Schopenhauer, behind the force that allows body movements, there's will, unfulfilled aspiration and without satisfaction of that desire, there would be no force so the world would "freeze".

Things are a bit different with conscious beings. When the will of a conscious being is prevented, it's struggling, suffering, and feeling pain until the obstacle is removed. If the obstacle is removed, then it keeps striving and striving, feeling emptiness and it has a feeling as if something's missing. Every aspiration as such, because it stems from the lack of something (otherwise it wouldn't be striving), is nothing else but suffering, pain, and agony. If that aspiration is directed towards some specific, concrete object, then it's prevented and it's suffering until it reaches the concrete object, until it's satisfied. If there is no object to which it's striving, if it's not prevented then it's a pure aspiration, a desire without its content but only itself aspiring just because it's aspiring. In that case conscious will feels desolateness, scarcity, pain which is different from the one caused by the prevention. Schopenhauer calls that type of unbearable pain – agony. For those reasons, some Heaven where all aspirations and wishes are satisfied can't exist as something beautiful but as desolateness, like suffering. Being of will doesn't consist of having but aspiring. Seeking to have is just an illusion, the will can only aspire. From that inner nature of the will, it's clear that any satisfaction can be only instantaneous, and that the feeling of satisfaction is basically nothing else but the absence of pain. Similar to the Epicureans, that satisfaction is of a negative nature. While pain is primary and realistic, satisfaction is secondary and imaginary.

Schopenhauer's claim that knowledge brings greater pain results from the fact that pain is felt, known as endurance. The greater knowledge is, the more suffering becomes known, the pain grows with knowledge. In unconscious inorganic nature, the will doesn't have the knowledge of its suffering, and it's similar to a plant, which, having no consciousness, can't feel suffering as pain. That already gives a hint that Schopenhauer will give a medicine for a trouble called life. Animals have consciousness and therefore feel pain. However, since animals aren't able to worry or anticipate the sad, unwanted, unfortunate future they suffer less than humans. It's comforting for a man to have hope, anticipation of a happy, desired future, which makes majority of life pleasures. But pains which are the results of failed hopes are extremely big and together with pains arising from worries and real pains of the present make the life of a man more unhappy and more painful than the life of an animal.

Human life moves between desire and satisfaction of the same, and desire is in its nature pain. Satisfaction of desire produces satiety, and the same occurs in another form, looking for some other contents. Even when a happy life is secured, we don't know what to do with it, so we strive to free ourselves from the burden of life, to kill time, to escape agony. Agony isn't easier than need in any way, because it can lead people to the same dissipation as need can. The last one is a whip of simple people while agony is of noble people. Pain is reduced as much as the distance between desire and satisfaction is reduced, but our desires are always bigger, and ways to satisfy them are few. Schopenhauer finds that aesthetic and intellectual satisfaction are the only lasting satisfactions but that they are available to very few people, while the vast majority of people are left with the delights of the senses. Health, food, moisture and cold protection, sexual satisfactions are the physical needs of animals as well and entire lifetime of humans is reduced to their satisfaction. If hunger ceases, need arises immediately either in the form of a disease or sexual instinct or unrequited love, fear, honesty, and many other painful forms. Schopenhauer believes that even if all those needs are satisfied, a terrible agony arises which brings a man to horror. All that we know about life and the history of people before us teaches us that this a priori logically deduced miserable nature of human's life, corresponds to the truth.

Besides that, we live in time and the only reality in time is the present, which is constantly passing, fleeting in fact; time itself reflects the nothingness of life. Such as it is, the world can't be the creation of some all-knowing, all powerful and all-embracing creator, a being who besides will has knowledge as well. How to understand that the all-powerful and all-embracing creator has created such a miserable and sad world that gives us more right to criticize and curse it than to praise and bless it. On the other hand, the pantheistic approach that sees the world as an eternal being makes the pain in it eternal as well. Thus, the world becomes a problem for a pantheist. Why should the world have such an amount and intensity of pain? According to Schopenhauer, both Theism and Pantheism have a groundlessly optimistic view of the world. What should we say for those optimists who see this world as good? This world is the worst of all possible worlds, and if it had been just a bit worse, it couldn't have existed. With this view and conclusion, Schopenhauer opposes Leibniz who believes that this world is the best of all possible worlds, since the creator, having in mind all possible worlds, made the best world due to his goodness.

Yet, Schopenhauer can't be right, since there are temporary pleasures in this world, and agony is still easier to endure than physical pain, while in the worst imaginable of all possible worlds there would be constant pain of the highest intensity and we don't see any principled reason why such a world couldn't exist. Some scientist, a psychopath could keep a man under narcosis, attached to electrodes, which stimulate all sensations in the victim's brain. There wouldn't be outside world for the victim, except for the one which is sensed by electric stimulation of the corresponding areas in brain. The demented scientist could also program stimuli to inflict constant pain on the victim.

In Schopenhauer's opinion, our life can't be understood in any other way but as an error, as a debt that needs to be paid out in great pains. That view has been expressed, as claimed by Schopenhauer, by three largest and most widespread religions - Brahmanism, Buddhism, and Christianity that teach that our life is the product of sin and that it must be destroyed to return to its original state where there's neither death nor agony and pain.

According to Schopenhauer's ethics, the essence of morality lies in compassion, which is quite consistent with his metaphysics.

The main ingredient of life is pain; therefore all moral activities must be directed against pain and suffering. Compassion stems from informing the individual that he's equalized with the other through the unity of the will itself. Both of them are only individual objectifications of the same will, so one can participate in the pain of another. All moral activities and all virtues with justice, love, and nobleness as three basic virtues stem from compassion.

The basic medicine that Schopenhauer offers for life full of suffering and pain is destruction of that will. Having realized that pain is associated with the will to life as a thing in itself, the individual understands that the only way to save himself from pain is to destroy that will to life. That destruction of the will to life can be achieved gradually through ascetic way of life. Schopenhauer rejects suicide, a sudden break of the will to life, because a suicide didn't reject the will to life as such, but only his empirical self. The suicide hasn't rejected his life because he has realized its misery and nothingness, but because his desire can't be satisfied. An ascetic, contrary to a suicide, starts his healing when a feeling of disgust begins growing in him, both towards himself and towards other beings, which causes such pain to the will to life. He strives to stop wanting anything that has attracted him including sexual instinct in the first place. Voluntary abstinence is the first step in leading an ascetic way of life or denial of the will to life. If that maxim of chastity would become general, human race would die out and Schopenhauer believes that fauna would be exterminated as well, since with the destruction of knowledge it would disappear into nothingness like the rest of the world, because there is no object without the subject of knowledge.

We have to notice that this idea is anthropo-solipsistic and it doesn't consider the possibility that after the extermination of the human race, some new sensible race that would suffer pain could evolve from animal species. If the will is thing in itself that already exists in inorganic substances and it has that essential trait to aspire, and to aspire even more if it's prevented, it would find a way again to incarnate itself into a conscious race. Schopenhauer also overestimates the power of an ascetic in relation to nature. An ascetic is nothing else but a slow suicide, because the denial of the will in him isn't enough to deny the will by itself.

Schopenhauer argues that asceticism is the only truly free event in the history of the world even if it isn't mentioned anywhere in history. An ascetic isn't the one who's conquering the world but the one who's surmounting it. He raises the question how is the phenomenon of asceticism even possible when human character is constant and not prone to change. How can people of different characters come to know the nothingness of the world and deny the world and themselves? Since knowledge in its course is independent of the will and it's external in relation to it, that knowledge of the nothingness of the world comes from the outside and it's the effect of grace, and the consequence of that grace, the denial of the will to life is rebirth.

With the disappearance of the will to live, our knowledge, which is the product of our will, also results in nothingness, which is the goal that the priest of Thulsa Doom mentions to Conan. Although Schopenhauer can't prove that the real world disappears with the denial of the will to life, from the point of view of his theory of knowledge, we can accept that the complete denial of will would also mean the disappearance of the world. Of course, there remains a problem how the disappearance of a man, the highest form of life, would also mean the disappearance of the world of suffering, when with the help of the will, as thing in itself, which remains despite the disappearance of the world of presentations, other forms of sensible life could evolve too. Perhaps the solution is that, as claimed by Schopenhauer, no higher form of life other than this of a human is needed.

The greatest knowledge that any race can reach is the one, which his philosophy has reached - that this world is eudemonistically negative and that conscious beings can't find and keep happiness. He doesn't need aliens, who wouldn't be able to tell us anything essentially new in case we get in touch with them. Schopenhauer's philosophy a priori rejects utilitarian goals of the greatest happiness of majority of people as impossibility. The amount of satisfaction in the world is fundamentally insufficient to annul the pain that the world produces with its essence of will that keeps striving, regardless of whether it's striving for some object of desire or just striving.

By negating the will or the will to life, we're defeating the world and it doesn't mean anything to us anymore. By extinguishing desires, and above all by overcoming our instincts, we attain peace, and in that peace we're welcoming death as long desired dreamless sleep, where no one will be able to disturb us anymore. Schopenhauer's philosophy is the basis of Buddhist teachings, various forms of Brahmanism and early Christianity. Besides that, it's logically more consistent, more radical and extreme thought that's behind those religious teachings. Basically, that's the attitude towards life, which is its negation.

In the case of Thulsa's pilgrims, besides that Schopenhauer's extreme attitude towards life, we still recognize hope, which isn't in line with the teachings of nothingness and emptiness that we hear in the words of Thulsa's priests. Those believers more resemble later Christians who're hoping for another, better life, and who don't accept that such a life logically, if we acknowledge Schopenhauer's philosophy, isn't possible. Those pilgrims even remind more of a herd, an amorphous mass of weak people, who are attracted, guided and exploited by charisma and the strong will of Thulsa Doom. In the following scenes when the Cimmerian's company manages to sneak into the habitation of that religious and military leader, we see which fuel that well-organized religious machine uses. That machine is oiled by the flesh of its followers. Cannibalism is the esoteric practice of the privileged circles of Doom's organization. The meat with which they feed themselves, they could get precisely from the bodies of believers, whose hopes in a better life they're using to fill their own stomachs. After the arrival of priests and priestesses in the pilgrimage camp, the believers are getting white clothes and they're moving in a line one behind the other, towards their place of dwelling, or should we better say to Thulsa Doom's feeding place, where they expect salvation.

ANTICHRIST CRUCIFIED

In Milius's artistic work, the meaning of the term antichrist isn't the same as Nietzsche's understanding of that term. Milus creates more human, it could be even said more Christian antichrist than that of Nietzsche. Although *Conan the Barbarian* has been inspired by Nietzsche's philosophy, whose significant feature is a sharp criticism of Christianity and which in its opus has a work precisely named *the Antichrist*, Milius's barbarian has been portrayed with some Christian trait, so the prefix anti in the compound noun antichrist can be translated rather as instead than anti-.

In order to understand Milius' antichrist, first we must understand Nietzsche's. After all, we can only be confused by the art presentation of Christ's crucifixion if we aren't familiar with Christian teachings. I remember that, when I have seen the crucifixion at my grandparents' house as a child, I couldn't understand what's the purpose of a presentation of a poor man in agony, and why would anyone keep that in his home in the first place.

Let's assume here that the reader is more or less familiar with the Christian teachings, since without that he can't understand the criticism of those teachings. We'll present the criticism on the next few pages. Nietzsche believes that Christianity is more harmful than any vice. According to Nietzsche, everything that encourages the will to power is good, the power itself, and everything that results from weakness is bad. Therefore, Christianity as a religion of the weak and unsuccessful must be something bad. The first principle of anti-Christian sympathy is that the weak and unsuccessful should perish and one should help them to do so. It's important to understand that Nietzsche believes that a man is only one phase in the creation of an "overman" and that, therefore, we need to overcome our human weaknesses, rather than create a religion out of them. According to biblical teachings, man is created in the image of God and as such, he's the culmination of creation. There can't be created anything that's more perfect than a man, because in that case God could get competition. The naive presentation of God, as something similar in its appearance to human being, can also be found in other religions too. In pagan Indo-European religions, Gods look like humans. Thus, Greek Gods have a physical appearance of humans, but they also have some human weaknesses as well. That philosophy has been already adopted by Greek philosophers. Xenophon says the Ethiopians claim that their Gods are flat-nosed and that they're dark while the Thracians say that their Gods are blue eyed and red haired, and if oxen, horses and lions had hands and could draw and create art works like human beings, they would draw the images of gods and they would draw their bodies similar to their own, so horses' gods would look like horses, gods of lions like lions and oxen' gods like oxen.[36] It's likely that if there were some other intelligent species in the universe, at a certain civilization level, their members in their religious presentations would have gods who would look like them. Of course, it's possible to imagine some intelligent race that hasn't felt the need for the development of religion.

An "overman" who needs to replace and surpass a man can't have similarities with a Christian man. Of course, it implies the diversity of spirit and not so much physical resemblance. Humanity isn't a development towards something better, stronger or higher. "Progress" is a modern false idea. The European of the nineteenth century, Nietzsche's contemporary, is below the level of the Renaissance European. Nietzsche believes that the good road that the Renaissance man has previously taken, has been ruined by Luther's action and revival of Christianity in its new form, which is even worse than Catholicism. Christianity, in its each new

---

[36] H. Diels *The Presocratics (originally Fragmente der Vorsokratiker)* , Naprijed, Zagreb, 1983, p. 133.

version, leads a war against a higher type of man. That religious teaching has taken the side of all the weak, worthless and unsuccessful. From opposing the instincts of sustaining a strong wellbeing, it has created an ideal. For all those values of the weak, Nietzsche uses a French term *décadence* (decadence) with the meaning of decline, decay, degeneration. A species is corrupted if it has lost its instincts. Compassion isn't a virtue; it's contrary to strong feelings that raise the energy of life; compassion is depressed: when one feels compassion he loses power; compassion is a practice of nihilism, denial of life. In every noble morality, compassion is a weakness. Compassion is the guardian of all the weak. Its name isn't nothingness, but that worldliness, true life or it's called nirvana, salvation and bliss. Nietzsche in his later works finds that Schopenhauer, who he once admired and regarded him as a higher type of man, has become due to compassion, the enemy of life. Compassion is one of the greatest virtues in Schopenhauer's philosophy and regarding that, this philosopher takes the side of Christianity.

Nietzsche finds that many philosophers, German ones primarily, are just a sort of priests. According to him, an idealist, someone with pure spirit, is just a slanderer and a poisoner of life. The instinct of a priest, theological instinct, can be discovered beyond various philosophies. It's a form of falsehood that prohibits reality to get a word in edgeways at any point. Everything that's the most harmful for life is called the truth; it's being encouraged, recognized and justified. Faculty of Protestant Theology at Tübingen, which among others attended even Schelling, Hölderlin and Hegel (who move away from Kant in their philosophy and move towards reconciliation with Christianity) is according to Nietzsche the educational institution of the Protestant church in Germany and the place of birth of German school of thoughts. German scholars are largely pastors and teachers' sons, so it's no wonder that this theological instinct exists in German philosophy. Also, we have to mention that Nietzsche's father was a pastor as well. They have also sensed in Kant's teaching what could support theological instinct. Kant's philosophy has left an open path to the two most notorious misconceptions. One is the true world - Nietzsche probably implies the existence of thing in itself, which we can't perceive according to Kant by the power of our cognitive faculties, and the other is the moral arrangement of the world.

We perceive the world in a way conditioned by the limitations of our cognitive apparatus. For example, we can't perceive the world outside, as Kant defines them, a priori forms (intuitions) of senses, time, and space but we can't claim that there's nothing outside time and space. This skeptical position opens possibilities to claim that there could be beings outside space and time. Thus, the other world, the true world, or God himself, remain as possibilities. Another misconception, Nietzsche thought, is moral as the essence of the world. That's manifested in Kant's teachings in many ways. We can see it in Kant's belief that even in the society consisted of devils, there must be some form of morality, which the author of *The Philosophy of Conan the Barbarian* finds very convincing.

That position achieves its climax in the postulates of the practical mind (practical in the sense of dealing with moral issues and not non-theoretical issues) which are improvable claims that we must accept in order to give meaning to morality. Those are the freedom of will, the immortality of the soul and the existence of God. Kant has successfully denied rational evidence of the existence of God based on, allegedly, logical reasons and, instead of logical reasons, he introduced the moral ones. God is needed as a guarantor of the moral arrangement of the world. We'll stop at some sort of Kant's moral test, which exists, as claimed by Nietzsche, in a shapeless form of categorical imperative. According to Nietzsche, the categorical imperative and the entire Kant's moral philosophy is an illusion that expresses the decay and disintegration of life. Virtue, duty, and goodness are the side paths that lead us into life's misery. Nietzsche disapproves the fact that the categorical imperative is valid for all, while the strongest laws of preservation and growth suggest that everyone creates his own categorical imperative. We'll explain Kant's categorical imperative to understand what bothers Nietzsche.

Kant has been under the impression of Newton's explanation of natural laws that are valid mandatory and generally. Mandatory and generally, or universally, means without exception in any part of the universe. Today, that seems normal to us, but in the past there were different opinions and Aristotle is the best example. Aristotle's physics is the longest valid physical paradigm, and as it has turned out later, it's mostly wrong. The Stageiran's explanations of the world were already doubted in the 16th century (Galileo Galilei) and until Newton's time Aristotle has already lost the reputation he had in ancient times and the Middle Ages. What distinguishes Aristotle from Newton is that there are different rules concerning the movement of objects in the sublunary sphere, under the Moon, and the other rules in the area of perfection, above the Moon. Newton's laws, as we have mentioned, are universal and valid for the whole universe. Kant believed that, like the universal action of Newton's laws and, above all, gravitation in physics, there must be something similar in morality. Morality must be universally valid. Newton's physical paradigm is based on mathematical principles. Kant also wanted morality that would be based formally. This philosopher has argued that morality can't be based on some descriptive content, material, empirical, such as, for example, moral feeling. Kant would agree with Nietzsche that compassion isn't moral in itself. Any content of morality would become morally acceptable if it passed through the form of a categorical imperative.

In the most famous version, the categorical imperative runs like this: *Act only according to that maxim whereby you can, at the same time, will that it should become a universal law.* This is a form, while different maxims are content. Those contents must be acceptable to all intelligent beings and must be valid without exception; or they must be universal. We'll show you on the example of compassion how it works. Let's imagine the following maxim: "I only sympathize with the members of my own people."

This maxim isn't moral because it's not universal. It doesn't comprise all intelligent beings. In Serbia, it's not so unusual to come across people who don't sympathize with their own people but they sympathize with other peoples. Such a maxim of activities isn't moral because it doesn't involve one's own people. It's not moral to sympathize with all intelligent beings because then we sympathize with criminals too. As this imperative is valid for all intelligent beings and many intelligent beings don't sympathize with criminals, then we must reject the last maxim as well. Therefore, compassion is a matter of emotions and not morality. The bad side of Kant's formalism is there hasn't been created the maxim that meets his strict criteria so far. He himself offered two maxims: "Do not lie" and "Do not make false promises." But many people, including myself believe that those maxims don't meet the strict criteria of the categorical imperative. Why wouldn't we lie, if we think it'll save us from a killer or rapist? Kant gives weak arguments regarding that issue, pretty much below his reputation.

There's a question what benefit we have of the categorical imperative if we can't positively determine what's moral. The benefit is that we can determine what's not moral and thus avoid being manipulated. Let's check, according to Kant's standard, whether the Hague Tribunal is a moral institution. The Hague Tribunal charges only the former Yugoslavia and Rwanda with crimes committed there, and, in doing so, it prosecutes only the Yugoslavs and the Rwandans. The member states of NATO, which have committed crimes in these territories, aren't in the scope of the court's jurisdiction in The Hague. Other wars, Iraq and Afghanistan, where people are fighting and committing crimes, aren't also in the scope of that court's jurisdiction. Although the tribunal has the technical capacity to prosecute other people apart from those it's currently dealing with, it doesn't do so. The Tribunal in The Hague isn't valid for all people (i.e. intelligent beings) without exception, hence the Hague Tribunal isn't a moral institution. Therefore, the verdicts reached by the Hague Tribunal don't have moral power. Someone who's been convicted in The

Hague, although he really is a criminal, is the victim of an immoral institution. Not to mention those who's been convicted but innocent. It would be different if the Hague Tribunal spread its power to all (people / intelligent beings). In that case, it would fulfill the condition of universality. Of course, there would still be disputable how impartially it applies its powers in practice.

It's necessary to explain another important issue related to Kant's ethics in order to return to Nietzsche. It's about the gap between *is* and *ought*. That gap is the biggest problem in morality and ethics. If I know certain facts, why should I act according to those facts? In case I know that something is immoral, why should I act morally; or let's put it like this: many people continue smoking even if they know that it's harmful; how can we convince them to stop with their harmful habit? Kant addresses the biggest problem in ethics in the following way. Since the moral law is stemming from my mind, and not some external authority, I have the duty to act according to it out of respect for it. The will that stems from duty bridges the gap between *is* and *ought*. At the same time, we must act out of duty regardless of the consequences. The consequences of our actions don't play any role in the morality of our ranks. If someone left us some money at his death's bed to give it to his children and we promised him that we'll do so, we mustn't break the promise under no conditions as long as we're technically able to keep it. At the same time, let's assume that the children of that gentleman are terribly irresponsible, ungrateful and mean people who'll squander that money in a second. On the other hand, we need that money for our mother's operation. If we take that money, we'll be immoral persons, regardless of the consequences of our action. It is our duty, respecting the maxim of not making false promises, to give the money to his ill-mannered children. That's the case that Nietzsche probably has in mind when criticizing the abstraction of duty in Kant's ethics and the general concept of duty.

What else does Nietzsche disapprove? Equality bothers him. According to Nietzsche, each person creates his own virtue, people aren't equal, and each nation has its own virtue. Nation disappears slowly if they replace their duty with the general concept of duty. That abstraction of Kant's formalism is life-threatening. After all, as long as Kant insists on his positive moral maxims, we can agree with Nietzsche. Not to lie while others are lying leads to a certain disaster. Except in the case of absolute power, if there's an all-powerful God, he can afford himself that luxury. On the other hand, if we take the categorical imperative as a test of moral content, then it's of great benefit. No one, except ourselves, can present us some political institution as moral, if it's not. Kant's formalism is a good defense against manipulation.

What's the most important regarding Nietzsche's attitude towards morality is the fact that he's an immoralist. He believes that (over) man is above moral principles of good and bad. However, his critique of Kant has a good point too. According to Nietzsche, there's passion beyond our ranks. The will to power is nothing more than the greatest passion and urge that all beings possess. Passion, desire or instincts are stronger than duty. Let's imagine a marriage formed out of passion between two people, the instinct to extend the species, love; and let's compare this marriage with the one formed out of the sense of duty. Let's picture a dead marriage without passion between spouses and where marital duties are done out of duty. Which marriage would you like? The passionate one or the one formed out of duty?

Nietzsche believes that such philosophies are lifeless. Christianity has even worse status. Christianity opposes life. Nietzsche compares people's (national, ethnic, tribal) and Christian God to show how the Christian God of the poor and weak has been born. The people who believe in themselves also have their own God. They respect in him the qualities that make them feel superior, their virtues. They project their feeling of power into the being who they can thank for their inner satisfaction. It's the religion of gratitude. That God is both good and bad. He can even hurt. What kind of God would he be if he wouldn't know anger, revenge, envy, mockery, slyness, violence? The Jewish God Yahweh is violent and vengeful, Hera is jealous, Mercury is cunning, Kali is bloodthirsty, and there are many more such examples. When people are breaking to pieces, when they're losing their hope for the future, when subjugation as something useful and the virtues of the subjugated penetrate into their consciousness, then their God must transform as well, says Nietzsche. Then he becomes cunning, fearful, humble, desiring to find inner peace, rejecting hatred, seeking mildness, even love of the enemy. He constantly moralizes, crawling in the cavity of every private virtue, becomes God for everyone, a private person, a cosmopolitan person. He used to present one people, the power of people, all that's aggressive in people's soul and their thirst for power, but now he is just good God. And there's no other alternative for Gods – either they're the will to power – and they'll exist as long as they're people's Gods – or they're weak in the position of power – and then they necessarily become good. The deity of decadence, cut off from his manliest virtues and instincts, necessarily becomes the God of physiologically handicapped, of the weak. They don't call themselves bad but good. God of their winners becomes Devil. Nietzsche criticizes Christian theologians, who believe that God's development from the Jewish people's God Yahweh to the Christian God, is a progress. It's just the opposite. When everything that's strong, heartily, lordly, removes from the notion of God, when he gradually degenerates into the symbol of the stick for the tired, into the salvation anchor for drowning people, when he becomes the God of the poor, the God of the sinful, the God of the sick, the predicate rescuer remains as the only divine predicate. The poor can be found everywhere and they need such God. The God who promises happiness in the other world becomes something more elusive, more faded; an ideal, pure spirit, an absolute, thing in itself. That idea of God is one of the most corrupt ideas of the God, which has developed on the Earth. He's the enemy of life, the natural will to live. God is the one who's the formula for vilification of this-worldly life and justification of every lie of that-worldly life. It's the God of nothingness, dedicated will to nothingness.[37]

All those mentioned nothingness's remind of another religion related to Christianity - Buddhism. Although Buddhism is one of the religions essentially opposing life, Nietzsche is so intoxicated with the hatred of Christianity that he even begins to praise Buddhism. We can notice in Buddhism a life of restraint, a hidden desire to return to the uterus.

That philosophical concept is expressed picturesquely in a Serbian curse addressed to the other person, and exclusively in the form of imperative. I'm sure that Nietzsche would be thrilled with the philosophical depth beyond that intellectual creation. It seems that terseness is the main feature of Serbian way of thinking. Although Serbian culture hasn't developed its own particular philosophy, and philosophy is the culmination of spiritual creation, it has been answering philosophical questions in poetry, proto philosophical way of discussing the philosophical problems, which, unlike Homeric epics, is characterized by minimalistic expression. The beginning of the famous poem about poor (by wealth, not by personality) nobleman and his misfortune: *Once there was a person*[38] is an example how, with the help of an "existential" predicate, with the minimal language material, a person is recognized by the highest human standards and the whole palette of positive meanings. We don't say deliberately the title of the poem, since we believe that the Serbian of an average education should know some of the most important verses of epic poetry[39].

---

[37] Nietzsche is surprised that the strong races of the northern Europe haven't rejected the Christian God. They haven't invented a new God in two thousand years; the God of life who will replace a nihilistic Christian God. It seems that Nietzsche, isn't aware that Christianity in northern Europe is present for much shorter time, and more importantly, Christianity is often introduced by force. It was hard both for the Norse people, the Slavs and the Balts to accept such a concept and the politics of Catholic expansionism that stood beyond it.

[38] A phrase which is hard to translate in English

[39] Banović Strahinja, explanation for english edition.

After all, in the homeland of western philosophy, everyone knew Homer.

Apart from that, highly appreciated, scope of human actions where Serbian culture greatly stands out there's an unrecognized and seemingly vulgar area of human achievements where the Serbs deal with philosophical problems. That activity, where the above-mentioned Serbian terseness of thoughts, meanings and expressions becomes prominent, is cursing, which belongs to that circle of human activity, which is usually considered as non-cultural. All the philosophical issues relating to that part of the Serbian culture (we still have to recognize that status as a substitute for philosophy) are already solved. That can be seen in a mild insult directed to those people, who understand certain intuitive truths more slowly, who don't grasp current phenomenological details; and who don't understand immediately the choices of metaphysical assumptions and ad hoc hypotheses, and it runs like this:"Don't philosophize!" As I've heard, only one people except the Serbs, use it and those are the Slavic people. However, let's get back to the final beginning and the simultaneous completion of the Serbian dialectic and its fine philosophical argumentation to the world's religious issues.

The essence of Buddhism can be seen in the first truth of Buddha's teaching concerning the overcoming of suffering. Birth is suffering, illness is suffering, death is suffering; sorrow and lamentation, pain, grief and despair are suffering; association with the loathed is suffering, dissociation from the loved is suffering, not to get what one wants is suffering. All five spiritual and physical components of a person are liable to suffering. Man's life is characterized by discomfort, dissatisfaction, and even occasional pleasant experiences, due to their temporality and transience, are the cause of suffering as well. People suffer when they are too hot or too cold, they suffer at the moment of their birth or when they're powerless; they suffer when they're ill and in the end they become senile and die. They suffer mentally when circumstances force them to be with someone they don't love, or something they don't want or if they separate them from those they're attached to. All earthly attachments (relations with other entities) lead to suffering and rebirth.

The other noble truth of Buddhism lies in the claim that craving is the cause of suffering. A person focuses on transient existence, and not on nirvana. The third truth is that the cessation of suffering is possible. The lack of desire leads to the end of suffering and we're liberated. Let's imagine that we're in love with someone who isn't in love with us. Instead of longing for the beloved person in vain, it's the best to quench our desire. In that way, love ceases and we are, I can't really say happy, but at peace. Happiness is also the cause of suffering, because when it ceases, the memory of happy moments makes us suffer. The fourth truth is reduced to the techniques of numbing the desire and avoiding pain, and that makes the practice of Buddhism. Nirvana - extinction - is the goal of Buddhism and represents a perfectly peaceful and enlightened state of consciousness where passions are numb. Nirvana is neither death nor the Kingdom of Heaven; the condition of nirvana is neither death, nor nirvana is destruction; neither nirvana is the state after death. Nirvana can be reached for life, as Buddha managed to achieve it, according to this teaching.

From all the above mentioned, we can conclude that Buddhism is a way of escaping life and everything that constitutes life. Passions, desires, hopes, fears, feeling of happiness, contentment and other contents of life are what Buddhism wants to eliminate. Buddhism is a religion for the living dead. Now we can understand how much Schopenhauer, whose philosophy we've been dealing with in the chapter called *The Land of Hippies and Being of Nirvana,* is close to Buddhism, and how much he actually analyzes those religious ideas in his philosophy.

Both Buddhism and Christianity reject this world for something else. However, Nietzsche finds that Buddhism is a more refined religion than Christianity. Buddhism comes after a century of intense philosophical pursuit. When Buddhism arises, the concept of God is already eliminated. Buddhism doesn't fight against sins but suffering. It left behind itself, which makes him profoundly different from Christianity, self-deception in moral terms – it's on the other side of good and evil. Spirituality and long existence in logical terms and procedures have damaged the instinct for (developing) personality in favor of the impersonal. Resentment isn't part of Buddha's teaching. Resentment or *ressentiment* is one of the key terms for understanding Nietzsche's interpretation of Christianity. Resentment is the feeling of malice and vengefulness that occurs in the weak, the poor and the miserable towards the strong, rich and happy. That feeling of malice and vengefulness isn't open but concealed. It unfolds in miserable persons by poisoning their souls. Resentment is the desire for something bad to happen to those who are happy. The strong people take revenge on their opponents openly and honestly. Resentment doesn't have that power; it relies on case, destiny, God. "God will punish them" – is the thought of the subdued person. The very idea of the Last Judgment where the God punishes the sinners (read: strong willed, passionate people, who are conquering the world or themselves) and rewards the good ones (read: weak-willed, mean people, the subdued, people escaping life) is nothing more than an eschatological, the idea of resentment which is finalized. Buddhism can also be a religion of the upper classes, while Christianity reveals the instincts of the subdued. Prayer maintains an affective relationship with the one in power called "God". There's cruelty towards oneself and the others (inquisition, asceticism). Christianity is hatred for the spirit, pride, boldness, freedom, freedom of the spirit; Christianity is hatred for the senses, the pleasure of the senses, joy in general, while in Buddhism there's only escape from joy and sensual pleasures. When Christianity, originating from the lowest layers of ancient civilization, came in touch with the barbarians, it used the barbarian's concepts and values to subdue the barbarians. The souls of the barbarians, contrary to those of the Buddhists, are strong but torn, eager to do misdeeds and spread their inner tensions in the enemies' ranks and presentations. Hence the significance of the stories of sacrificing the firstborn child, blood drinking in Communion, contempt of the spirit and culture, torture in all forms - physical and mental. Buddhism is a religion for the generations of people refined by civilization, mild, kind, liable to pain. Buddhism is a religion for the end and fatigue of civilization. Such Nietzsche's views might imply that Christianity is more pro-life than Buddhism, which doesn't support his argument that Christianity opposes life.

Nietzsche further argues that this religion of the weak has evolved from the unfortunate fate of Israel. In the times of kings, the God meant being conscious of power and later due to anarchy and the pressure of the Assyrians, the idea of him changed; he could no longer achieve what he could earlier, he was no longer one with Israel, he becomes the God of Justice. He becomes a tool in the hands of priests - agitators who interpret luck as a reward, and each misfortune as a punishment for disobedience to God, as "sin." That's the falsest way of interpreting quasi "moral world order" where the idea of causes and consequences is reversed. Through reward and punishment, natural causality has been expelled from the world. Thus, moral has become abstract and anti-life. Jewish priests falsified the history of Israel and turned it into the tool of salvation. The feeling of guilt according to Jehovah - punishment, devotion to Jehovah - reward. Unfortunately, the philosophers have agreed to that too. On such a false ground, where every natural value, every reality, had the deepest instincts of the ruling class against itself, Christianity developed. The rebellious movement, which is once again the Jewish instinct, a priestly instinct that no longer tolerates a priest as a reality, an even more derived form of existence, an even more unrealistic vision of the world than the one conditioned by the organization of a church. Christianity denies the church. According to Nietzsche, the rebellion was probably directed against the Jewish church, against the hierarchy, the caste, the order. The attack on it was the attack on the hardiest people's instincts, the most resisting will to live that ever existed on the Earth. Christ, the anarchist of the Jewish society of the 1st century, died due to his own guilt; there's no basis that he died due to the guilt of someone else. Nietzsche also believes that Christianity has falsified Christ. Kingdom of Heaven is a state of heart – it doesn't come from "the above" or "after death". Christ doesn't resist, he doesn't defend his rights before judges, cops, slanders and mockeries. He doesn't take any step to avoid the inevitable, he challenges it, he loves it with those, in those, who are inflicting harm on him. Don't defend yourself, don't fight, don't be responsible, don't resist evil – love it! Nietzsche believed that there was only one Christian and that one died on the cross.

After that accident, there was a riddle before his followers "who was he and what was he?" The possibility that his death meant the end of everything they believed in, was too distressing for them. Everything had to get its higher purpose since the followers' love doesn't recognize coincidence. The highest class of the ruling Jews were accused of that. And how could have God allowed that? The absurd question got an absurd answer: God sacrificed his son for the forgiveness of sins. A sacrifice for a debt, "the sacrifice of the innocent one for the sins of the guilty! What horrible paganism!"[40] - argued Nietzsche. Later, "bliss" - a state of the Spirit of Nazareth and the point of the Gospel -is hidden for the benefit of the state after death. A completely opposite type to "good messenger" (Gospel means good news), genius in hatred, in the vision of hatred, in ungrateful logic of hatred, is embodied in Paul. Paul is a priest who wanted power again. He could gain it by concepts, doctrines, symbols used to tyrannize masses and create herds. What did Muhammad later borrow from Christianity?; Paul's invention - belief in immortality i.e., the teaching about judgment.

When the focus of life moves to that -worldly life - to nothingness – life disappears. Further, Nietzsche disapproves

---

[40] Nietzsche, Friedrich 2002: *Antihrist* , Dereta, Belgrade, p. 140.

breaking of natural laws in Christianity for everyone. Everyone has the right to salvation, no matter how miserable and worthless he is. "Equal rights for all" is a poisonous teaching that Christianity has rooted. Aristocratic mentality was undermined by lying about the equality of souls. Nietzsche quotes several quotations from the Gospel to show what those worthless people believed in, and we'll quote here only one: "And he said to them, "Truly, I say to you, there are some standing here who will not taste death until they see the kingdom of God after it has come with power." A lion told a convincing lie.[41] Nietzsche also quotes the following words of Paul: "God has chosen what is weak in this world, foolish in this world, not noble in this world and the despised." Christianity is the supranational victory of all the weak and miserable - the faith of the deprived. The believer is necessarily an addict who can't set any goal for himself. The spirit that's great is necessarily skeptical; liberation from all kinds of convictions is the power of spirit. Nietzsche compares Christianity with Manu's Code of Law, which he takes as well designed spiritual work that distinguished philosophers and warriors use to subdue the masses. According to Nietzsche it would be a sin to make it equal with the Bible. It summarizes experience, wisdom, positive verified morality, concludes and it doesn't add anything. It doesn't give reasons and causation since thus it would lose its imperative tone "you should", the assumption of its respect. Nietzsche believes that the whole effort of the ancient world was in vain due to Christianity. He argues that the base for great culture was already built back then; the scientific methods were established, the ability to read, the sense of facts, the development of mechanics and mathematics. He says that Christianity is a great curse, the greatest internal corruption, a great instinct for vengeance where no means are poisonous enough, secretive, underground - the immortal shame of humanity.

---

[41] Ibidem, p. 145.

We've seen from all the above that Nietzsche really doesn't appreciate Christianity and that he opposes it. He's setting different standards for one higher race. To what extent does Milius's Barbarian meet those standards and where does he move away from them? Is war and courage more than love for one's fellow humans?

Within the main concept of Millius's Barbarian, the traits of a higher type of man can be seen. The very selection of an actor who'll play the main role speaks for itself. Arnold Schwarzenegger looks like the will to power that has been transformed into flesh. With his patient, intense work, inspiration, out of spite towards his father, that will converted into one extraordinary life. Schwarzenegger is a man who has won his first title Mr. Universe at the age of 23, which makes him the youngest bodybuilder who has won that title. Already as a young man, he himself has foreseen his own destiny- that he would become a successful Hollywood actor. He has won the title of Mr. Olympia for seven times. During the shooting of the film, Conan the Barbarian got an amazing body shape because of riding, running and fencing, and he wanted to apply for the eighth time, but due to an accident at the training he gave up. The role of Conan the Barbarian was the turnover in his career; that film made him a star. It's interesting and maybe even fate for a person of such will and "unrealistic" ambitions to achieve success, precisely in a work of art based on the philosophy that takes the will to power as the basis of reality. Just like Conan, after countless adventures, acquires political power, becoming the King, Arnold Schwarzenegger achieves similar success. This film star has become the governor of one of the most developed USA state with a share of 12% in the total population of the USA, i.e. it has the same number of residents as Spain, one of the largest European countries. It's most likely that the film about Conan the Barbarian hasn't been filmed earlier because there was no actor who would convincingly interpret him with his body.

It's incredible that those two works of art coincide. We believe that Arnold Schwarzenegger's body is a work of art as well. Bodybuilding is the unrecognized art of the 20th century. Even before, people used to build their bodies. In ancient Rome, wealthy people who had free time, proper diet, trainers and weights, used to do it. They liked to go to public baths to gloat in front of the poor, who mostly had weak constitution. In the 20th century, due to the general growth of standards, bodybuilding became mass art. The closest to bodybuilding out of recognized arts is ancient sculpting. The sculptor of that period is trying to carve the perfect body in stone, taking care of every cut he's making with chisel, since in the final stage of the creation; one error can cost him all his previous work. However, once he finishes his work and hands it over to the purchaser, the sculptor is tranquil because only fate can ruin his product; nothing depends on him anymore.

Bodybuilder is in a more difficult situation, because he himself is both the artist and the art. If a bodybuilder makes a mistake in building his body, he can't leave it and start again. Bodybuilder works only on one project his entire life, and his work is transient; it lasts much shorter than stone. Today, the body of Arnold Schwarzenegger, the most successful artist in bodybuilding, has lost its tonus. The effort of an artist building a body is greater than that of a sculptor; he feels tenser; tense as the muscles of his body in the competition. They are both inspired but body demiurge must have stronger will. He has to give up the food he likes, the sculptor doesn't have to, and the body creator has to practice regularly, because if he relaxes, muscles become loose. The sculptor can give up his art for several years, and then return to it with even more inspiration. Besides that, he can work on his projects as an old man too. The creator of his own body has a limited time to achieve success. After some time, no effort or experience helps him. In the future, his experience can be useful for the others but not for himself. It's true that we shouldn't reject the possibility that the development of medicine will significantly increase life expectancy and period of youth of human body. Thus, the works of that art will last longer. By comparing those artists, all the time we had in mind the top representatives of both disciplines who are willing to sacrifice all to their success. In conclusion, we should bear in mind that Milius has chosen for the role of his *Barbarian* a man of an iron will, who is an artist both as a builder and actor and whose entire life is a work of art.

Regarding that, it's striking that Conan the Barbarian has a constitution opposite to that of Christ. In art, Christ is presented as a skinny, sometimes almost starving ascetic. As if the artistic presentation of Christ corresponds to the later interpretation of his teaching as a critique of this world and the promise of another, eternal and beautiful world. Giotto, known for his title *the volume master* given to him by critics at the beginning of the 20th century, has painted Christ crucified as a person who was starving for a long time. (Santa Maria Novella, Florence) With his skinny arms, visible ribs, large stomach, resembling paintings of hungry people from the time of the great drought in Ethiopia in the 1980s, with unhealthy greenish skin color, Christ seems as if he had been on bread and water for years, before being crucified. In Dürer's painting *Adoration of the Holy Trinity* Christ is colored with more vivid colors, in line with the colors of the whole picture, but he still looks skinny and weak. In Max Beckmann's *Descent from the Cross,* Christ looks like a prisoner of war. As if the painting represented the victim of the Holocaust and not the savior. That painting has been created under the influence of Grünewald who has often used the theme of crucifixion in his work. Grünewald's painting displayed in Washington *The Small Crucifixion* shows extremely tortured and skinny Christ. Although Christ isn't always skeletal in art, that tendency is always present, and he generally looks skinny. There were many painters, sculptors and engravers who liked to deal with that theme. There isn't any historical reason for such presentations. Christ spent relatively short time in a dungeon. According to the teaching, he was tortured, and later crucified. Torture and cruelty were preceded by the trial by Jewish priests, where he was found guilty of blasphemy. Later, he was handed over to the Roman prefect Pontius Pilate who was interrogating him, and allegedly, according to tradition, which says that one prisoner should be released before the feast of Pesach, he offered the crowd to choose between Christ and Barabbas and decide which one will be released. The crowd chose Barabbas.

It seems that Christ in art doesn't represent himself but all the poor of this world. We've noticed earlier that there is an anthropocentricity in the understanding and presentation of gods in many religions, in Christianity there's the same tendency, but of one class of people. All those miserable and poor people of this world are presented in many paintings of Crucifixion. It's a simple psychological explanation according to which we project our traits on the other person. Another reason may be the desire to show Christ's sacrifice as greater as possible. The skinny, starving body seems as if it has gone through many troubles of this world. That explanation seems convincing. There's another more interesting explanation. Christ doesn't like to consume this world, he remains alive by using the most essential. Perhaps a good taste prevents him from doing so? How can he enjoy the taste of this world when he knows what it's like to be in the other world? That adds some eminence to Christ that Nietzsche wouldn't accept easily. Thus, this world is shown to be truly inferior, and according to Nietzsche it's the only world that exists very and that's valuable. However, presenting Christ's body as skeletal, indicates on certain distance to this world. Perhaps Nietzsche's right, perhaps Christ is a blissful, listless being who can be tolerant, although his behavior in the temple of God towards money changers whose tables he overthrew, doesn't fit that image of him. Such an act isn't a trait of a mild person who can endure much. Regardless of the explanation of such Christ's representation in art, we can't be fully satisfied. Christ hasn't written anything and we can only know him through mediators, which leads to serious problems. The historical Jesus will always remain a secret.

We can comfort ourselves with the opposite situation that we have at our disposal regarding the crucifixion of the Antichrist. We can interpret Conan's crucifixion because we have evidence of the teaching about the antichrist. Nevertheless, there's a shadow that covers the antichrist. He's not genuine, he's a substitution. Even Milius's artistic antichrist is created from a series of references to Christ. Conan is caught and interrogated by Thulsa Doom's follower. The Barbarian was proclaimed an unbeliever, just as Christ was proclaimed a blasphemer. Although, there's a difference, because an unbeliever is also a skeptic and here Conan matches one of the features of Nietzsche's antichrist. Christ is a rebel within a paradigm, a religious view of the world. The danger to Jewish priests consists in the competitiveness of Christ, as a religious leader, and in Christianity as a competitive religion. Similar reasons have brought about to the conflict within Christianity. The fight for political positions. That's how the Eastern and Western churches separated. We mustn't be deceived by alleged reasons related to the doctrines of Christianity, the main conflict is of political nature. Therefore, the struggle for power is the cause of the separation. There's a similar situation with Protestantism as well. Protestants are fighting for a political right to have the Bible in their own language and to be independent of the Vatican. It's strange that Nietzsche hasn't noticed that there's the same tendency beyond the Protestant movement as well; the aspiration which he finds dominant among all beings. Nietzsche is simply blinded by hatred for Christianity.

However, let's get back to the Barbarian. He is an unbeliever and as such, he brings into question the priests, in this case Thulsa Doom, in a more dangerous way. They're superfluous for him. He doesn't need religion. It's true that he does have his God Crom, but his attitude towards this God is ambivalent. He could do quite well without him as well. After all, he doesn't do any rituals, he doesn't offer him any sacrifices. He speaks to him only once, for the first time, seeking help in getting his revenge. He ends his short speech with a curse addressed to his God. Conan isn't religious. Crom is his God because of the tradition. He's more of a proverb or prop - word than the God. Conan mostly relies on himself in life.

Nonetheless, Milius puts him in a similar situation to that of Christ. He's being tortured and interrogated. The hearing is done by Thulsa Doom personally. We can see the traces of torture on the Barbarian's body, and he's shown in torn clothes similar to Christ. Unlike Christ, Conan is accused only of his sins, and he has his own mission. The Cimmerian is also sentenced to crucifixion. Unlike Christ who was crucified on the cross, the Barbarian is tied to the tree of pain. Due to the film ending itself or out of the respect for Schwarzenegger's work of art, Milius hasn't desecrated the Barbarian's body. The Barbarian's crucifixion itself is the opposite of Christ's representation we've been dealing with. Conan is muscular, he represents the will that doesn't count on the other world. It's true that Millius has shifted from Nietzsche. The director has created the other world. And that other world is Valhalla; it's the world that recognizes the struggle and courage. Valhalla isn't the heaven of the equal. In that view, Milius approaches Nietzsche. Valhalla is the heaven for the best, for warrior aristocracy, for the brave and successful. Milius has moved away from Nietzsche's "overman", which is a term equivalent to the antichrist, in the fact that his "overman" is also a barbarian. Nietzsche doesn't have a high opinion of uneducated people, and that's the feature of barbarians. Nietzsche's "higher" type is brave as much as cultured. His "higher" type is enriched by an artistic instinct. Milius himself approaches him in that field. Here we're bearing in mind that it's questionable whether Nietzsche would recognize bodybuilding as an art.

Conan, crucified on the tree of pain, doesn't recognize defeat. He pretends to be weak to attract a vulture, which he kills with his strong teeth. The will to life bursts from every Barbarian's molecule. From every inch of his healthy body tissue. At the end, a friend saves him from the tree and the Barbarian goes through something similar to pagan resurrection. Conan is already experiencing clinical death until he falls into the arms of his sweetheart. At that point, the "overman" again approaches the Christian theme of the resurrection. Due to the pagan rituals, and not the intervention of the Christian God, Conan "resurrects". We mustn't forget that there's love beyond his resurrection. One of the Christian main doctrines is also present in the antichrist. Although here, that love is expressed in the fight against demons, nature, destiny.

We've seen in this chapter that, apart from the theme of "overman", based on Nietzsche's anti-Christian values, Milius moves away from Nietzsche and creates a more human being. This deviation is the most evident in the part of the film when the Cimmerian acquires freedom. After a superb military training, Conan is a killing machine that his lord rents to those who are interested. On one occasion, they are sitting in the tent of some probably Mongol tribes with warriors. The chief of that tribe or tribe alliance, maybe Khan, fearing that his children will never understand him, asks the gathered people what's best in life. Conan gives the answer, which Khan likes: "To crush your enemies, see them driven before you, and to hear the lamentation of their women!" Later that night, during the witching hour, the master of the Cimmerian comes and cuts Conan's chains while saying to him: "Go, you're free!" In that scene, Conan really looks like some half-wild creature that's used to the life in chains and Schwarzenegger acts brilliantly Conan's confusion. His master, regarding the Barbarian as some being that's too much dehumanized, decides to give him freedom. That animal, non – compassionate feature that has evolved in the slave consciousness of this war machine, is something that could be qualified according to Nietzsche's philosophy as good. We can see the biggest difference in Milius's and Nietzsche's "overman" in the part of the film which we've quoted and retold. Milius's "overman" doesn't exist and can't be more than a man without an ingredient called compassion. True, that's presented indirectly through Conan's master, but it's clear that the director doesn't want to build his "overman" without the feeling of compassion.

127

SNAKE IN HEAVEN

There are several important reasons why the sequel to *Conan the Barbarian*, under the title *Conan the Destroyer*, isn't as good as the first part. In the first chapter, we've mentioned the example that shows that it's not "well shot",i.e. it isn't at the same technical level with Conan the Barbarian. Of course, technical knowledge is necessary but not sufficient in making a good movie or other work of art. Many directors have technical skills and make average, sometimes even good films, but they don't create masterpieces such as *Citizen Kane* for example.

We haven't accidentally chosen that achievement by Orson Welles. There are some similarities between the Barbarian and Citizen Kane. Welles has made that film by introducing various technical innovations, but the film isn't a masterpiece due to that. Welles, in a subtle way, by portraying the life of, by external standards, a successful man, who has achieved an American dream, suggests that there are values more important than wealth and the recognition by the others.

Rich Kane has lost his childhood and all his life he's been trying unsuccessfully to compensate that grievous loss. Despite all his power and wealth he remains miserable until his death. This movie presents morality in an unobtrusive way. That unobtrusiveness itself, leaving to us to draw conclusions and interpret the work of art, is an important ingredient in the recipe for creating masterpieces.

Conan has suffered a similar loss. The Barbarian's loss is even more severe because, apart from his childhood, he has irreversibly lost his family, his people and the world he's known until then. Unlike the previous example, the Cimmerian has the advantage of being able to hate a particular person and direct his frustrations towards negating the one who has caused his misery.

That testifies to the fact that a good story must satisfy, and by that the above average movie differs from some average movies. Creating an authentic bad guy is a tested recipe for the success of a movie. In many works, we can hardly imagine the entire realization without the contribution of bad guys with their persuasiveness and charisma. Would the fairy tale *Star Wars* be so successful without Darth Vader? Not only would that film achievement be damaged, but it would be half-empty if the creators of that work hadn't created such a successful bad guy. After all, parts that have been shot afterwards deal with Anakin Skywalker's youth and the motives that have turned him to the dark side. Darth Vader carries the entire epic.

What significantly contributes to the success of *Conan the Barbarian* is the existence of a successful bad guy. Interestingly, James Earl Jones, who plays Thulsa Doom, the bad guy in *Conan the Barbarian*, has given voice to Darth Vader. The deep voice with the characteristic accent, which passes through the microphone, supported by the sound of breathing helped by an artificial device, makes the characteristic feature of Darth Vader without which his role as a potent dark personification of evil is unthinkable. In Conan the Barbarian, we can see Darth Vader BC. The demigod, which possesses the human and animal form of snake, one of the most detested animals in many cultures and especially in the European, is an essential ingredient in the film achievement that we're analyzing. In the unsuccessful sequel of this achievement, there's no such a bad guy that can match the depth and authenticity of Thulsa Doom. Perhaps it's because *Conan the Destroyer* is primarily movie for kids, so therefore, besides an authentic bad guy, there aren't any particularly bloody scenes with which the first part abounds. Not to mention that we can guess the ending already at the very beginning of the movie.

In creating Thulsa Doom, Milius has perhaps referred to the famous *Old Man of the Mountain*, the story of Marco Polo. It's about a sect leader who, according to Polo's story, owns magic gardens full of pretty girls. He drugs his followers, puts them to sleep, and then transfers them to those magic gardens. Then he wakes them up, explaining to them that they are in Heaven and that if they serve him well, they will stay permanently there after their death. Later, he puts them to sleep again and transfers them to the real world. After that experience, they are supposed to be faithful to death and willing to do anything that the sect leader asks them to do, including suicide. Then, the old man from the mountain has used them to carry out assassinations of political figures for him. The word "assassin", which used to refer to the Islamic sect from the Middle East, has changed its meaning into killer i.e. assassin since the period when Marco Polo's story has become popular.

There aren't any historical confirmations for that story. The name *assassins,* which was first used in Syria, was given by the Crusaders to the followers of the Ismaelite Nizarite sect. The name derives from the Arabic word *hashish* (hashishin) which means Indian hemp, used as a intoxicant within this sect, which the Europeans have adjusted to themselves. The conflicts of the Crusaders with those people holding important hill fortresses in Syria were frequent.

The very fact that Thulsa Doom has chosen the mountain as the place of his living reminds of the story *The Old Man of the Mountain*. The main trait that brings him closer to the old man from the myth is that he's presented as a charismatic religious military leader, who draws his strength from his ability to manipulate people. He always uses present human fears and problems to use people. Besides the natural charisma required for leadership, he also possesses a supernatural trait that suits the snake aspect of his nature - the ability to hypnotize his prey. We see that his ability for the first time in the scene where he kills Conan's mother (when he unexpectedly manages to lower the guard of the Barbarian's mother to cut off her head in a cold blooded way) and all that to the eyes of young Conan. Later in the movie, he tries to use the same ability against the adult Cimmerian.

It's perhaps pointless to wonder what type of a man Thulsa Doom is, since he's only half human, but that question is still open. He's a kind of a man, who is ready to do anything to increase his power. He belongs to Nietzsche's "overman" as well. When he was a bit younger he was trying to answer the riddle of steel. On the transition from the Bronze Age to the Iron Age, the revolution that took place in the metallurgy, regarding the manufacture of steel weapons, brought considerable advantage to the owners of swords and other weapons made of that material.[42] The Celts managed to rule over the large part of Europe with the help of that metal in the 1st millennium BC. Naturally, Thulsa Doom embarked on a venture that would bring him military supremacy, unaware that he sealed his own destiny with his trip to Cimmeria and the destruction of Conan's village. There's some doubt regarding that venture related to Thulsa Doom. In the part of the movie where Conan's trying to infiltrate the ranks of Doom's followers, the mountain is shown with a monumental staircase dominating the environment. Pilgrims fill the stairs and the plateau in front of them. Thulsa Doom addresses the believers, letting them know that he's been watching them for thousands of years. He could be telling the truth since afterall he's a demigod. However, in the scene where he's questioning Conan, he remembers the destruction of the Cimmerian's village and he replies to Conan that he was younger then and he didn't realize that the real power doesn't lie in steel but in flesh. Has it taken a demigod, who's been living for thousands of years, a couple of decades of the Cimmerian life to realize that power over people is more important than power over metal? It seems that despite being a demigod, he has a human life span and a short time to understand how this world works.

---

[42] Iron can be found in nature more often than copper, which is an additional advantage.

Based on the size, complexity and success of his sect, we can see that he still understands very well how this world works. That villain has his own small army, but as we've noted earlier, that isn't what gives him real power. His charisma, which helps him to gather followers and seduce the mass, is the true source of his power. He's the type of leader who's more similar to Adolf Hitler or Winston Churchill than Stalin or Tito. Adolf Hitler was a man who felt the fears and needs of the German mass, which he managed to persuade verbally to obey his will. After all, the ending of the film, when Thulsa Doom gives a speech to the assembled followers at night, while they're carrying burning torches, reminds of German National Socialists meetings. Winston Churchill was also the type of a leader who, through his power of verbal (including literary expression) persuasion, was accomplishing his goals.

On the other hand, Stalin and Tito, who weren't eloquent people, pursued their intentions by simply eliminating political competitors in inter-party conflicts. But all of them used the problems of ordinary people to come to power and keep it. All of them use the trait of ordinary people who believe in the possibility of a radical change in the world, which will bring a permanent life quality improvement. If the masses realized that there couldn'tbe some fundamental change in the world (due to eternally limited resources suitable for creation of reason and rational behavior), there could be a solution that would alleviate human misery, even though the essential problem - human inequality – would remain forever.

Equality in distribution would cause dismantling social resources to pieces with which nothing serious could be accomplished. It's necessary to accumulate a part of social capital to fund any research endeavor, no matter whether it's a quest for new medicine, new territories or a new technological process. Few people can make decisions concerning that part of social capital, so that inequality is intrinsic to any form of social organization, be it humans or aliens. After all, if equality were possible, all humans would be literally biologically equal. The reality is different and people have different predispositions. We'll deal with those issues later. Now, we'll get back to Thulsa Doom.

We've seen that Milius in creating that character could have had in mind as a role model the old man from the mountain, a military, political, religious leader from the Middle East from the Middle Ages. There's another character who has served him as an inspiration in creating Thulsa Doom. It's Satan. According to Christian myth, Satan is a fallen angel and an evil competitor to God. When he discovered that God would create a new being - a man (toward whom he would direct his love), he devised a plan how to inhibit God's intentions. The first people, Adam and Eve lived in Heaven, a place where all their needs were satisfied. However, they weren't allowed to take fruits from the tree of knowledge. Satan sneaked into Heaven and took the form of a serpent. He succeeded in persuading Eve to pick the fruit from the tree of knowledge and share it with Adam. When they tasted the fruit, Adam and Eve learned what shame was and everything else they shouldn't have known, and the good God punished them by expelling them from Heaven. Besides that, they became mortal and had to suffer all their lives. Also, Satan is someone who tests the faith of Christ and offers him alternative options if he joins him. The shape of a snake isn't something that Satan has accidentally taken but his permanent feature. It's interesting that when Conan and his companions get into the mountain caves, inhabited by Thulsa Doom and his followers, they're under the impression that they've come to Paradise. At the moment when he turns into a snake, Thulsa Doom is sitting in the place with an artistic presentation of a tree behind him. There's an undoubted association between Satan and him.

Snake and tree are symbols of Canaanite religion. The Canaanites were pre-Israelite inhabitants, who were partly exterminated and partly assimilated by the Jews. At the time of the conquest of Cannan, the Jews were barbarians and the bearers of a distinctly male religion. Contrary to that, the

Canaanites belonged to the circle of Mediterranean civilizations strongly influenced by the female deity, i.e. a mother goddess. Many Jews were inclined to celebrate the female deities of the previous inhabitants, so Jewish priests fought against those cults by equating a snake with evil. The story about the expulsion from Heaven blames serpent and woman, the symbol and bearer of the previous religion. Unlike religions that were created under the influence of Judaism, such as Christianity and Islam where Priests are men and God is a male creator of the world, in previous religions that were spread over the Mediterranean area, i.e. female religions, priestly duties were performed by women. Besides the phallic explanation of snake's existence in religion, in those matriarchal religions, snake is associated with the symbol of the underworld, rebirth and wisdom. The serpent had originally ruled the oracle at Delphi until Apollo (the solar male deity who was brought to Greece by the Barbarians who conquered the weakened civilization by previous female cults and the matrilineal system) killed and appropriated the oracle. In Greek mythology as well, serpent is often symbolically associated with woman. Cassandra is given the power of prophecy by serpents, which symbolically clean her ears. There's also Medusa, an evil woman who has snakes instead of hair. Serpent, as a symbol of Mediterranean urban civilizations under female leadership (in Crete, Neolithic urban civilization was under the full leadership of women), with the political, religious and economic rise of men, becomes the symbol of evil, Satan. The symbol of bull is also associated with female religions. In Greek myths, a holy female bull is transformed into an evil monster - Minotaur, logically located in Crete. In Christianity, the devil is presented as a creature with horns, hooves and tail.

Thulsa Doom is a mixture of Satan, Hitler, and the Old man of the Mountain, but his main role in the plot is that he represents the point around which the Barbarian's personality will condense (if we believe that external influences are of greater value than genetics). Would the Barbarian exist at all, such as he is (a fearless warrior who subordinates all to his will to accomplish his goal) if it wasn't for Thulsa Doom? Is it perhaps Conan's normal character, an entelechy that's just seeking some kind of external impetus to manifest itself to the fullest? Perhaps character determines a man's fate, as Heraclitus thought?

Anyway, Thulsa Doom is trying to use his manipulative, hypnotic skills on the Cimmerian. After the crucial battle where the Barbarian's small group defeats Doom's elite forces, villain Doom retreats to his mountain. However, without his elite forces, Thulsa Doom is unable to physically protect himself against the persistent Barbarian, who reminds of the ancient Terminator. Naturally, it's no wonder that there's similarity since it's the same actor with a different styling. In the part of the movie where the final fight takes place, we see that the herd, seduced by Doom, isn't able to protect him. Think about that if you ever wish to go into politics. Thulsa Doom's trying to protect himself and turns the matter to his advantage using his rare gift of verbal persuasion.

Doom says to Conan: "My child, you have come to me, my son. For who now is your father if it is not me? I am the wellspring from which you flow. When I am gone, you will have never been. What would your world be, without me? (he lays his hand on his shoulder while looking Conan straight in the eyes) - my son." - he tells him that with a very suggestive look. At that moment, Conan becomes confused, turns his gaze away and looks down, beginning to think; isn't all that Doom is saying true? Isn't Doom actually the Cimmerian's spiritual father, the point around which the Cimmerian's life revolves? Isn't Doom the cause of the Barbarian's identity? Won't Conan suddenly find himself faced with the gaping chasm of the emptiness of his own being, whose one side is Doom himself? For a moment, the Barbarian is challenged by Doom's understanding of Conan's soul, his knowledge of the consequences of the Cimmerian's life choices. Doom is a cunning snake that understands people better than they understand themselves. All that was said so far about Doom wasn't that important for the successful creation of that bad guy as much as the words which we've just quoted, but we don't know whether they were written by Milius, Oliver Stone (a screenwriter) or the unsigned Edward Summer. Those words alone show how deep soul that being possesses. From those words, we understand Doom as a person who has lived through all human fears and made all human decisions suffering their consequences. That snake has consumed human soul just as ordinary snakes consume an egg. All the content of a human soul with all its worries and hopes has been refined in Doom's personality. This superhuman being uses all the doubts, weaknesses, expectations and fears for the future to break the resistance of a man's spirit: persistently, subtly, gradually like water breaks down rocks, only much faster. It dissolves human will as a highly concentrated acid of understanding, support, forgiveness and salvation. That wise being knows the answers to unasked questions, but latently present in the unconscious mind, beneath the thick crust of denial, self-delusion, and delay. His very spirit is like a snake, wrapping itself around a human soul, pressing it, drowning it but injecting a sedative that relieves the primal horror and makes the loss of breath invisible.

But human spirit possesses something that allows it to defend itself against manipulation. Spirit rests on foundations that are indestructible in some people. The primordial basis of human soul which created consciousness, the kind of intelligence that man shares with beasts, and which Nietzsche unusually appreciates, is instinct. Instinct is a cure for manipulation, and according to Nietzsche, an "overman" is the barbarian with unbreakable instincts. At no other moment does Milius's Barbarian correspond more to Nietzsche's "overman" than when his instincts wake him from the paralysis where his own reason has led him to, helped by Doom's instructions.

At the moment when the camera looks away from the knocked out Cimmerian, and focuses on his followers as they stand below, they're already inferior by their physical position to Doom and we observe a mass of broken wills, a herd tamed by his powers. When the camera returns to the Cimmerian, we see that his instincts have overcome the short circuit that Doom has caused in Conan's bioelectric circuits and we can notice how the instinct's spark has returned the glow to the Barbarian's spirit. He swung his sword and killed Doom, before the very eyes of his terrified followers. They are retreating, going backwards in fear of pain. With every blow of the Barbarian's sword, they let out cries, while the Barbarian commits one form of Freudian patricide, only without feeling guilty later or having problems with the unconscious.

Holding the head of their leader in his hand, Conan slowly walks toward the crowd. With each step he makes, the music celebrates his power. To the pilgrims, that herd of souls with depressed wills, the unbroken will approaches, which is supported by unbreakable instincts that are chosen to withstand the pressure of nature and society during millions of years; instincts that have been skewed by civilization and reason in pilgrims.

When the pilgrims slowly parted, we find the Barbarian in a pose, seemingly atypical of the barbarians. Contemplative Conan is in the pose of a thinker, typical of philosophers, men of science and great inventors. Why has Milius placed Conan in that philosophical pose?

Doom himself gave the answer to that. Having achieved his goal, the Cimmerian is faced with the fundamental question of life: what now? Having accomplished his amazing epic mission; having received recognition and getting his revenge, Conan asks the same question as Tyler Durden (Brad Pitt) in the movie *Fight Club*. While talking with the other half of his personality (in Edward Norton's interpretation), Tyler points to the essential emptiness and meaninglessness of life. He did everything his father had expected him to do, and after graduating from college, he asked his father the question: "What now?" However, he could not get the answer that could satisfy him. The movie *Fight Club* gives the same Nietzsche's answer to questions about the meaning of life as *Conan the Barbarian* does. According to the philosophically most profound analysis of this world (that of Schopenhauer), Conan found himself in the following situation: His will has been inhibited from his childhood. The Barbarian's muscles have been created to fulfill the function of desire of Conan's being. That desire basically included the liquidation of Thulsa Doom. However, with the fulfillment of desire, there's a void, and the will continues to aspire into the void, feeling miserable. Fight Club shows agony caused by consumer society. It constantly produces new desires that we can't satisfy making us thus permanently miserable. Even when they succeed in satisfying certain desires, wise people face nothingness because at one point they realize that satisfying individual desires doesn't bring happiness and they reject the totality of such culture. The solution to which the characters of *the Fight Club* are resorting to is fight, and even more, adventure. In the movie, civilization is portrayed as an inhumane monster that grinds down masculinity. This artistic insight is very deep, and we just have to remember all those civilizations that have been possessed by the barbarians, if not already destroyed by them. Civilization necessarily tends to fulfill women's needs and interests and destroy the men who need to defend it. This film portrays well the impotence of civilized man.

Conan the Barbarian metaphorically shows the way to recover strength. We've already mentioned that the wizard, Conan's chronicler, lives near the megalithic artifacts because the fire has burned out in that holy place. After the battle and the tragic death of the brave female warrior - Conan's sweetheart, the Cimmerian group arranges her funeral on the stone altar inside this monumental building. However, the pyre prepared for the female warrior burns contrary to the wizard's experience. This flame shouldn't be interpreted other than as a metaphor for the potency of the warrior lifestyle. Heroism, which the ancient gods admire and demonstrated by the Cimmerian group, is a classic form of showing sexual power, an instinct that exists as the basis of the living world. Nature without masculinity can't be fertile, and civilizations are dying out because they've managed to castrate the masculinity that should fertilize them. One only has to take a look at the ancient hippies, as portrayed by Milius, and we'll see that the label "masculine" can't be attached to them. We don't understand masculinity in other way than as will, and it doesn't have to exist only in the way as it exists in the strong body of Conan the Barbarian. Weak bodies can be containers of strong will too. Gods have allowed the fire to burn because they've been amused by a good fight, and they value war and courage. Gods respect Conan and they sympathize with his loss. They want people like him. War doesn't have to be an armed conflict, as shown in the movie. Sports competition, economic war, competition in the market, the fight of opinion between different thinkers and all other competitive activities are indicators of masculinity. War, as an armed conflict is the toughest test, but it doesn't have to be inevitable.

At the end of this chapter, we'll notice that despite the fantastic interpretation by James Earl Jones, Thulsa Doom isn't in the top 50 of the American Film Academy's best villains. We believe this is an injustice, which this book aims to to fix at least a bit.

PART TWO – BARBARIANS

SEXUALITY AND IMMORALITY

In this part of the book *The Philosophy of Conan the Barbarian* you'll find out why beauty won't save the world and why women love bad guys. This part of the book is the most important and its goal is to overcome the problems of Kant's deontological ethics and Nietzsche's immorality by giving some solutions that provide morality which can be applied to life but which is at the same time formally correct. In order to solve this issue, we have to state certain problems arising from male-female relationships. At some point, philosophy started dealing with that problem (Heraclitus is credited with claiming that there are special male and female morality), but it has moved in a different direction. Issues related to this topic remained unsolved and unchallenged.

In dealing with this problem, we'll have to tackle human sexuality. Humans are a species that possesses a certain quality related to breeding, which is common with many other species. It's sexual reproduction. We'll leave the explanation of the occurrence of sexuality to another philosophical work, which is in preparation. We'll single out, as essential for sexual reproduction, the specialization that arises within a species. Man has the quality of transferring information through his semen, which is very small in size when compared to a considerably large egg cell. As if the quality of woman is to store energy in the form of an egg. The cyclical nature of menstruation when the egg, if unfertilized, dies, is parallel to cyclical processes in nature. On the other hand, there's no cyclicality regarding the fertility of male semen. It seems that man plays the role of a synchronizer between the cycle of woman and the cycle of nature.

To define man and woman, we'll use the functions they perform in the struggle for survival. First, we'll use only natural selection and sexual selection to outline and explain the traits of "ideal" specimens of the species. Later, we'll add more resolution to the understanding of masculinity and femininity by applying the main idea of a synthetic theory of evolution that's prevalent today. Then, we'll make some observations regarding the aesthetic ideals of the human species, and finally we'll explain why there can't be unique morality for women and men, explaining the point of patriarchal morality. We'll also try to synthesize Kant's formalism and Nietzsche's immorality and present our version of plebeian and aristocratic moralities, which are much different from that of Nietzsche, but using his idea of the existence of two morals as a role model.

There's a joke that says that men are divided into good and bad suppliers. This joke is a step away from the truth. In the biggest part of human evolution, men have taken the role of acquiring resources for survival. Those resources were taken and immediately consumed or stored for later use by women. We could say, drawing a parallel to the joke with which we've started this paragraph, that women are also divided into big and small consumers. It's logical for men and women who give offspring (and we're primarily interested in them) to give a significant part of the acquired resources to their offspring. Women have a strong maternal instinct that entirely directs many women to take care of children, to that extent that they're ready to significantly threaten or end their own survival, just to give children a chance to survive. Naturally, there's a greater possibility that women with stronger maternal instincts will give offspring. This particular maternal instinct plays a crucial role in choosing the right man. From the potential mother's point of view, the main qualities of the right man are independence, power or social status, and only then there are qualities related to his physical appearance. To speak the truth, there are women that don't match our ideal, but we'll deal with them later.

Independence means the ability to take care of oneself and to depend as little as possible on the other person. Naturally, that implies good health. A person without good health depends on the others who take care of him and he spends his resources unproductively. Besides that, he isn't able to contribute to the community and to his potential wife and children. Therefore, healthy men are more sexually attractive to women, and vice versa, women's health is attractive to men. White skin color appears to be widespread for reasons of sexual partner's health diagnosis. A girl's white skin color easily indicates if a girl is anemic. In case she is, which makes her less able to bear pregnancy, she'll have a noticeable pale complexion, and in case she's healthy, she'll have more blushing face. If skin is dark, such changes are more difficult to notice. By choosing light-skinned girls, men gave their biological successors an epistemic advantage that allowed for more rational sexual selection. The hypothesis that white skin color has been transferred through a species through men's sexual selection, is confirmed by the fact that European white men are on average darker than women. There was also the influence of the environment, which through natural or external selection depending on the society, preferred white color due to the synthesis of vitamin D in a low light environment. Yet, we believe that the reason was sexual selection to the great extent.

Another important meaning of independence is separation from parents. In hunter-gatherer communities that took a huge chunk of human evolution, it was certain that a hunter who wasn't even capable of catching enough food for himself, wouldn't be the choice of a potential mother. In modern societies, women prefer men who aren't dependent on their parents as they have proven their provider skills.

Henry Kissinger, Nixon's foreign minister, once said: "Power is the greatest aphrodisiac". It's the great truth. Powerful men are desirable. However, what makes a man powerful? Is rich man more powerful just by that fact? That's often the case in some cultures, such as modern liberal-democratic-capitalist cultures. Yet, it seems that it isn't enough to define power through wealth. In warrior cultures, wealth isn't enough; it's more important to be skillful in a fight. Party leaders in parliamentary democracies can become more powerful than the wealthiest men. After all, would we say that Warren Buffett or Bill Gates are the most powerful Americans? Many people believe that the secret services are those with the real power. Personal wealth in cultures that strive to be egalitarian isn't essential. Then what can we say about ordinary people? How does a woman evaluate an ordinary man? How does she make a selection from that group of men? What defines a real man?

It's typical of man to have a close relationship with nature. In one sense, it means hunting and physical labor, and in another, it means that man comprehends nature directly. The gentler half of our species learns about nature indirectly through the male fruits of physical and intellectual labor, whereby in the hunting part of our evolution physical and intellectual effort have been synthesized. Scientific research has shown that men are better oriented in physical space and time. Natural laws, the physical world, mathematics, astrophysics, relations between physical bodies in space and time are all men's job when it comes to knowledge. The relationship with nature is crucial for the function of a man within the species. Natural selection leaves in life and gives the possibility for reproduction to those men who manage to master nature itself. Aristotle tried to define a man as a reasonable animal whereby man's function is to act in line with reason. We can agree on that. Nature is the object of knowledge and it leaves in life those who live in harmony with it.

There's one range of interaction between nature and man that escapes woman's reason. Nature reveals its rules to the man of its choice. It fertilizes man as man fertilizes woman. In some cases, the fascination with nature and its beauty decreases and dulls the interest in woman. Newton, perhaps the greatest mind in history when it comes to formulating physical laws, didn't seem to have any interest in women. He was completely captivated by nature like Andersen's Snow Queen, leaving no warmth for women in his heart. It's important to note here that there's no evidence that Newton had sexual intercourses with the same sex.

Kant is similar to Newton in those matters. For Kant, natural beauty is the only true beauty. True, he appreciates works of art, but natural beauty comes first. Even in visual arts, he appreciates forms such as arabesque or other motives that don't present people. We have to notice that even gay artists are able to convey the beauty of a woman's face and body, but Kant, like Newton, doesn't seem to belong to the merry population since he's so in love with nature. That sorceress also cooled his heart against the opposite sex. His ideas of cognition are entirely directed to nature, even when he directs cognitive problems from nature to man himself. We bear in mind that he's dealing with a cognitive apparatus by which we know nature, not the awareness of society, which is the product of a man. He doesn't believe that time and space are real entities but forms of observation that we have before any empirical cognitive experience. According to him, all of our knowledge is determined by categories regulating our sensory information. We can't learn thing-in-itself, nature itself otherwise than regulated by our cognition apparatus. There's something that we're missing, perhaps something that excites Kant so much that he doesn't pay attention to women. There's a question, which we'll answer later: is it enough for man to discover nature or should he find out something about women as well?

It's logical that nature itself determined the way we discover it. It has allowed us to find out enough to survive, and a bit more than that. Knowledge of nature has been essential for the survival of man. But what kind of knowledge has been vital for woman? Are there any female powers of judgment that are different from the male ones? Knowledge of nature and its principles has been critical for man, and knowledge of society and its creator-man has been crucial for woman.

We can draw a parallel with Kant's "Copernican Turn", where he, instead of knowledge of nature, emphasizes the power of knowledge by putting at the center of our considerations the way woman learns about society, i.e. a man. Certainly, evolution in women has created an a priori form that subdivides different cultural contents and life situations into certain patterns. We, men can't know directly what women's perception of ourselves looks like, but still, we aren't without tools for our cognitive enterprise. Although we can't penetrate female mind directly, we can observe female behavior.

The first thing we've noticed about man is that he discovers nature in an epistemically privileged way that escapes woman. We mustn't conclude that women have been denied due to that. Man learns from his relationship with nature how to get resources, while woman learns how to get the resources that man extracted from nature.The relationship between woman and man is similar to the relationship between flora and fauna. We are used to thinking that the animal world is at a higher level of development than that of plants. The world of plants has one characteristic similar to that of man - it has a direct relationship with inorganic nature. Vegetation draws resources directly from inorganic matter; on the other hand fauna uses plants for its nutrition and indirectly obtains resources for its survival.

Woman uses man like animals use plants, so we have to ask one fundamental philosophical question. If woman doesn't need to know much about nature because nature-related tasks are performed by man, does this mean that woman's intelligence is at a higher level of development in a qualitative sense? Is all man's knowledge of nature actually for the purpose of woman's needs? Here we have to mention an important truth not to be misled on the wrong path on this issue. Frances Bacon believed that knowledge is power and it's a popular half-truth. Knowledge is important but insufficient to gain power. What's the point in knowing the truth if we can't do anything about it? In many cases knowledge is totally useless. What benefit does a fly have of knowing that it'll be eaten by a spider? Isn't a sick man's knowledge of the cure for his illness worthless if he can't get it due to the number of circumstances? Take the example of our hero Conan when they bring him and make him sit near the battlefield opposite his opponent. The Barbarian doesn't know what it's all about, and he remains seated with an undisturbed peace of mind. The knowledge that he would fight to death with the man opposite him wouldn't bring him anything useful. He couldn't escape since he's been chained and he would only be upset for no reason.

Similar to that is the cognitive power of woman. A particular woman may well know that beauty is something that could have an effect on man, but since she isn't attractive enough (let's assume that her other qualities aren't enough for that man), such knowledge doesn't bring her any benefit. It can only make her suffer. Our point is that knowledge doesn't necessarily bring power, and if we proved that women were more intelligent beings than men, it wouldn't mean that they're dominant. After all, reason develops precisely in those beings who are limited in some other ways in reaching their goals, so they use intelligence to compensate for their deficiency.Woman is physically inferior to man (bear in mind that we're talking about the ideal types of man and woman) and she can't impose her will using her physical power, as men did during evolution, and they do today in certain situations. Woman compensates her physical weakness for the special type of cognitive powers that have evolved in line with the biological function of woman.

It seems that aesthetics for woman when choosing a man is entirely subordinated to reason and that there's no room for liking without interest. Here we also include the part of the reason buried into our unconscious. When choosing woman, man is guided above all by physical appearance, the beauty of a woman, which can't be placed in some clear and unambiguous definitions. Of course, science has made a lot of progress in determining what defines a beauty in a woman. Thus, estrogen is known to give certain features that attract men, such as large eyes. Also, Dr. Stephen Marquardt has discovered the universal facial beauty rules that can be applied to almost all cultures, and it's essentially defined by golden ratio. But still, there's something that can't be defined. Thus, according to golden ratio, Florence Colgate was named the most beautiful girl in Britain in 2012. Although Florence is really beautiful, you'll agree that many would think that there are more beautiful girls that they personally know.

The author of this book will give examples from his personal experience to illustrate that female ideals of beauty are easily defined. I'm sure that readers have such experiences that will help us to understand, through the method of observing women's behavior, at least externally, their cognitive system. Observing women's behavior is one of the most easily applicable observations in social sciences and can be applied on a day-to-day basis, on the simple condition that there are women and men present. Also, this observation can be done by anyone without investing in observation equipment. Everyone can check the claims made about women in this book as a neutral observer of a statistically significant sample in mixed societies. Of course, facts depend on theory, so they should be regarded from this book's point of view.

Already in famous 1993, which is known in Serbia for monetary hyperinflation and lack of resources for ordinary people, one spring day, I was having coffee with a female friend in a neighborhood when her female friend honored us with her presence. I was still young at the time and I naively assumed that the same standards of sexual attraction can be applied both to men and women. An attractive friend of my friend was excited because she met "a hot guy". I expected, due to my inexperience, that she would start describing some handsome guy, but she started describing him together with hand gestures: "He has a gold cross this big, on a gold chain!" Clearly, physical appearance meant nothing to her, but the "tough guys' status symbol" said all about the guy she was interested in/ meant a whole lot to her.

I'll mention another event to show the wisdom of millions of years old evolution. And that wisdom attracts women towards successful men. We use the term successful as a synonym for a powerful, rich man with social status, a leader and all that defines the success of a man given his biological function within the species. Many women aren't sincere when verbally stating the qualities of a man they're attracted to, pretending that factors such as wealth and social status aren't important to them. This verbal smoke screen can't hide their behavior, which give them away. My humble self had lucky eye-opening circumstance to sit with an honest woman in Strahinjic Ban Street in Belgrade a few years ago. While we were sitting in one of the cafes in the street, an attractive young lady kept turning her head and looking at expensive cars passing by and at one point she said:"They're cute, even when they're ugly, they're cute." It's the right example when the reason takes over the judgments of beauty. To be honest, I have to admit that the above mentioned girl had the intention to hurt the feelings of this book's author for reasons that are inappropriate to state in books like this, but that doesn't cast the shadow of a doubt on the sincerity of her above - quoted words.

Such truths aren't new for many men, but there's an astonishingly high percentage of the stronger sex members, who don't accept reality, and those examples, besides very young people, are meant towards them as well.

Regarding knowledge, as we've already noted, we assume that woman possesses an a priori form of perception of social status, regardless of experience under the coverage of empirical content. Woman evaluates man's social status based on some factors such as an expensive car, branded clothes, an area where he lives etc. Just like man manages well in space and time, woman manages well in social relations. There's another, even more important criterion, which we don't know where to establish.Is it the same form of perception or is it a completely new power? It's the evaluation of a person's status depending on his relationship with other men. Be it a hunter-gatherer society, warrior, theocratic, trade, Marxist, national-socialist, democratic, liberal-democratic, state-capitalist society etc, there's a hierarchy among men. The strength of a man springs from a group. In order to understand that in the right way, we must first understand why group has become prominent in human evolution.

Group can defend itself more easily. It's not the same if you are being hit by one pair of hands or hooves or if you are being beaten by a half a dozen of them. Group defense had more advantages at the time when human ancestors weren't predators yet and when they lived in a relative paradise where food could be picked from a tree. When the climate in Southeast Africa, the cradle of humanity, changed (it doesn't change anything even if it had hapenned elsewhere), the rainforests began to disappear, giving way to savannahs, and our ancestors had to provide food that they couldn't get anymore just by stretching out their hand. A herbivore became a carnivore hunter. Since primates aren't particularly fast animals, their evolution couldn't have taken easily the path, which for example, "domestic" cats that hunt independently thanks to their speed have taken. Group hunting could bring results only by simply surrounding a prey, which then couldn't easily escape. A group makes better use of space and time. An individual can't be present in several places at once, while group, by dividing the roles of all individual males in the attack or defense, overcomes that problem.

Also, it's easier to catch large animals in a group. Hunters can attack a surrounded animal from multiple directions alternately, making the defending animal constantly engaged, thus bringing it to the point when it collapses due to fatigue. We'll mention that in humans the ability to regulate heat by sweating has become a key factor in hunting, besides group and tools. Animals, such as antelope, must cool themselves either by simply finding tree shade or by tongue dangling, which serves as a cooler in a way. Human ancestors were getting rid of the excess heat by sweating, and then compensated for the loss of fluid by simply drinking water. That allowed hunters, by carrying enough water with them, to follow the antelope until it collapsed, and then they would kill it. This example will serve us to show the effect of natural selection and sexual selection.

A hunter who has gained this advantage regarding body cooling has been able to endure more exertion than others and impose himself as a leader. Needless to know the technical reason which has made him a leader, women had sexual intercourses with him more often than with the others, transferring his useful genes further. After several generations, the whole group had a new useful quality that increased their chances of survival. The group of hunters was now becoming even more efficient in hunting, allowing the development of other organs such as brain through a larger amount of meat. After all, water cooling itself helped brain, which consumes proportionally the most energy out of all organs, to work better. Also, we should note that many women find attractive the qualities of men which were created by that selection in the hunter-gatherer era. And vice versa.

Many other species of both herbivores and carnivores survive in a group - buffaloes, antelopes, dogs, hyenas, etc. Within a group, individuals can alternate in performing certain functions, thus saving the energy of whole group. Falling asleep outdoors would make them an easy prey but within a group a guard function can be done on shifts.

A group needs someone to lead it in order to act harmoniously and coordinated and to obtain optimum results. To become a leader in any species isn't an easy job, but it allows you to be the first one to mate with the best, or all the present females, as our ancestor who first had water cooling did. It helped him to impose himself as a leader. In some cases you're the only one who has sexual intercourses. Female logic is simple - if other males have recognized you as the best, there's nothing left for women to study - they want the best themselves. Women can easily rank the place of a man in the hierarchy. Still, nature gives the final judgment. The fact that the others have recognized you as a leader doesn't mean anything if nature doesn't leave you alive.

The above mentioned problem, which shows the limitations of the feminine cognitive apparatus, is a critical problem of the feminine cognition power. This feminine cognitive apparatus is set to detect within intersocial relations and external factors that can change the balance of powers within the society most often escape the epistemic powers of women. Mutations such as water cooling don't happen often and people with abilities that aren't necessarily evolutionarily useful become group leaders. They aren't sometimes useful at all or they're based on luck. Let's take the following example from modern period.

A young, attractive girl who wants to get married and have children or in a less ambitious case she just wants to have fun, has chosen a man who suits her due to his success. He's relatively young business leader who has his own developed business and he imports raw materials for some technological processes in the manufacturing industry. Let's say that he imports food preservatives for a food industry, with a number of employees who depend on him, and he can afford high standard of living for his young chosen one. That couple has been living a life worth living until, alas, the raw material, which the guy has been importing, became totally useless due to the technological breakthrough in production. With new technological processes, preservatives are no longer needed in food production. All his success has been based on luck. After all, it was also the case with his ancestor with water-cooling who can't take the credit for the genetic mutation he got. Our young businessman tries to compensate for that loss by importing other goods, but the market for those goods is saturated and those business arrangements prove to be unsuccessful. Losses follow one another and the businessmen can hardly be called successful. After a while, he can't any longer provide to his chosen one the life she is used to, and she suffers the consequences of her cognitive limitations regarding the knowledge outside the social world. She couldn't have predicted that changes related to man's relationship with nature would make the product of her chosen one superfluous. She acted like her ancestor, who didn't know the real reason behind the success of the leader with a useful mutation that made him an alpha male. She's simply chosen the one that's been more successful than other men, with a higher social score. That's what contributes to woman's genes.

Now, we're reaching the crucial way how women overcome their cognitive limitations regarding nature. What remains as a possibility for a woman, if she's still attractive enough, is to look for another successful man who will provide new resources for her. Whether a woman already has children or she plans to have them, by her choice she actually supports the chances for her children to survive and have a good starting position. Many people, both men and women influenced by patriarchal morality, would conclude that this woman is an immoral person. The writer of this work must stand up for the woman in the example for the following reasons.

We've seen in the previous part of the book that there are situations with energy crises ranging from economic crises to catastrophic famine when the members of society at the same time come into situations where holding to some humanistic moral ideals would lead to certain collapse. In the shipwreck dilemma, we've shown in a logical and consistent way that if we want to survive, we come into a situation where we have to suspend our moral norms. The mere suspension of moral norms undermines the universal validity of morality. An additional problem is that various people face energy crises daily, such as the woman and her chosen one in the example. Many of us are faced with lots of such situations where moral behavior could ruin us during our lives. The woman in the example we've discussed wishes her children well and we can't blame her. After all, what has she done badly? She may have deluded her chosen one that she loves him more than anything else. The worst she could have done was lying to him, and according to some people that makes her immoral. We'll check later whether lying itself is immoral.

Some nations come into situations when holding to morality in international relations would only bring them trouble. Japan attacked the United States in 1941 because the Japanese power elite thought that their competitor would block their oil supply and make them go back to the way of life which they led before industrial revolution. Starting a war with the US, provided that their information was accurate or just assuming that they believed it to be true, can't be considered immoral. In case that they misinterpreted the information they had, we could see the beginning of that war as a tragedy, not just immoral act.[43]

Let's get back to woman now. Cognitive abilities of a woman are superior to those of a man in a specific way. As long as there's a society, a woman will be able to evaluate men correctly. As long as there are people, there will be money, i.e. high status men. Only in case of the collapse of society, i.e. species, women's cognitive powers become excessive, but then nothing can be done anyway. To the extent of their validity, women's cognitive abilities are principally perfect. Still, they can always be more perfect in some technical sense related to education, experience or other circumstances.

The case of communist China, where wearing the same blue uniforms was obligatory for all, is also interesting. The women were able to judge who managers were, based on the cut and quality of the blue uniforms material. Even in pathologically

---

[43]It's interesting that the Japanese garrison in New Guinea in World War II, due to Japanese General Staff misjudgment, got into the shipwreck dilemma. Thousands of Japanese soldiers found themselves in a situation of starving to death or resorting to cannibalism due to the lack of food, caused by the poor judgment of the generals. Not only did they eat dead and captured Allied soldiers (whose flesh they were cutting off bit by bit in some cases, because if they had killed them, their flesh would have gone off quickly in a warm climate), but also later, they were drawing lots to decide who they would kill among themselves. It's clear that if they had held to their usual morality, no one would have survived that situation .So, morality has a limited domain. There are situations where it's inapplicable. That's why it can't be universal.

egalitarian societies such as Communist China, someone had to organize and synchronize the activity of the group, i.e. society, and therefore that person got a slightly bigger piece of pie, just a bit bigger, but sufficient for women to detect it.

This could be the right moment to answer the question whether a man must possess knowledge of women. There's a common saying "Who can understand women?", which testifies to the essential men's misunderstanding of women's motives. We believe that the fact that men generally don't understand women prove that it wasn't crucial to understand them to leave offspring. For man, it was important to understand nature and get something from it, while for woman, it was important to understand man and get something from him. At first sight, it isn't necessary to understand woman in order to leave offspring. However, as we'll see later, not knowing the consequences which women's independence leave on group, leads to the collapse of entire civilizations. This is one of the most important new truths revealed in this book.

First, we'll talk about the main advantage of sexual reproduction. We've noticed that woman has an egg, i.e. child, as the main value of the species. Woman behaves conservatively, like a bank that shouldn't lend money to anyone. If it invested in everyone, it would fail, like it was the case with the banks that initiated (though they didn't cause) the global economic crisis, because they neglected selection in the race for profit. By the way, we must mention that saving those banks was an extremely anti-market act. A woman who wants to have children can't risk like the above mentioned banks even though the position of a woman in society is analogous to that of a bank in the economy. A bank invests stored energy of its depositors, expressed in money (here we mean some real money that's backed up by some real value which also isn't prone to inflatory raises in value as it is the case nowadays with fiat currencies), in risk-taking businesses that have an analogous function to that of a man in natural selection. A bank can't know in advance which business will become successful. The business that starts producing results will increase the amount of money in the account. The bank will detect it and invest the deposited money of its depositors in a successful company. In that way, the bank's shareholders will ensure profit, i.e. survival.

Woman treats man in a similar way. Woman can't know in advance which man will become successful. She'll be able to choose a posteriori, only when some of those men start to pump resources into society. That may explain why women generally prefer (4-5 years) older men. Older men had time to succeed. Since the number of successful men, i.e. leadership positions, is relatively small, there are more women to one successful man, so men come into the situation to make sexual selection too. A woman has an egg where she stores energy, i.e matter, while a man, chosen by nature, has information in his seed related to what nature has approved.

Men, as one sex of the species, are determined to take the risk. Many men won't be able to survive and prove themselves as successful in conquering nature. They won't even manage to survive. Most of them won't succeed in achieving some success. But the sexual function of a man is such that one who succeeds can fertilize more women and thus easily transfer the right (which means in line with nature) information regarding how to conquer nature to offspring. Einstein believed that God doesn't roll the dice, and we can conclude that it isn't the woman who is prone to roll the dice. Man takes the risk for her. In this way the entire species protects itself from losses and increases the number of options.

We can draw important conclusions from this gender specialization that determines the specific functions of woman and man. One of the conclusion is that Dostoyevsky wasn't right when he predicted that beauty would save the world. If all men were handsome it wouldn't do any good to the species. Man's task is to be successful, not beautiful. Women would still prefer successful to handsome men. On the other hand, if all women were beautiful the situation would be more difficult for less successful men.

Successful men can limit their choices to beautiful women in the present situation, leaving some less beautiful women to less successful men. If all women were pretty, which one would remain to some ordinary man? Of course, we've simplified matters and carried to extremes in order to prove our hypothesis. For most people, intelligence and character traits always play a significant role when choosing a partner.

The second conclusion is the following one. If nature leaves successful men alive, shouldn't only they breed? In *Conan the Barbarian*, they act according to that logic. Although a slave, the Barbarian has proven to be an excellent specimen in terms of strong mind and strong body.Therefore, in one scene in the movie, they bring to him excellent female specimens to pass around his genes. The problem with that is that we can rarely know which men are really successful in nature conquering. That's why liberalism in sexual selection is the most acceptable. There's another important reason and now it's time to introduce the main idea of the synthetic theory of evolution. According to this modern theory, evolutionists don't only observe individuals going through natural selection and sexual selection, but they rather concentrate on individual genes and their distribution within a species or a part of the population. An individual gene can spread quickly through a population if it proves to be useful. The other gene can reduce its presence. The fact that there are genes that skip generations and which don't always activate, isn't without significance. There are also recessive genes. In order to be activated, they must be present in at least one of your mother's parents and one of your father's parents. What's essential to us regarding this approach is that there aren't ideal woman and man in the species, and that the genes of certain traits are concentrated in one sex, but also they're present in the population of the opposite sex. In fact, there's a small number of particularly male and female genes, and sex dimorphism is created by having the same genes run a different program depending on the xx or xy combination of the chromosomes. Thus, besides the ideal types of man and woman, there are individuals who show the traits of genes of the opposite sex. In fact, that's the case with most men and women. This can be useful both for individuals and species.Thus, for example, some man can be more cautious than an average man who is more prone to take risks than an average woman, and he can increase the range of situations where men, the group or himself can survive. And vice versa. A woman who takes a risk can increase her chances of success compared to other women by choosing a man whom some average woman considers a weirdo.

Since in species such as ours, there's a large number of individuals across a large area in different climates and in different cultures due to evolutionary success in terms of humans' dominance in number and power over nature across the planet, some specialization has taken place.

Marx doesn't recognize specialization, since he believes that people have equal opportunities, but scientific knowledge and experience itself speak against it. One doesn't have to be a genius to notice that, depending on the climate, natural selection goes in the direction of the distribution of certain genes. Dark skin is present in warm areas since in that way skin defends itself against the burning sun. Other ways of defense against the Sun are also probably possible, for example genetic engineering, but nature already had its own word based on the genetic options it had. Genes that store fat deposits spread in a cold climate. This isn't only the case with the Inuit, but even more with other species of mammals and birds that live in cold climates such as seals, whales and penguins.

Culture or the way how some group of people acquire resources, effects the spread of certain genes, i.e. sexual preferences as well. Beauty ideals are determined by the way in which some culture obtain resources. In hunter - warrior cultures, there was a tendency toward a muscular body. For those who were fighting on their feet the emphasis was on their height, as was the case with Vikings (more specifically Norse people), while for people who were fighting on their horses lower body weight was an advantage. Generally in warrior cultures, woman's slimness is more appreciated. Poets of many ruling castes, of hunter-warrior origin stress slimness in women. A person should be able to reach the place and escape and naturally fat deposits don't help. For people who are more prone to peaceful problem-solving, lower muscularity and higher fat energy reserves improve the likelihood of survival during energy crisis periods. Muscular warriors would simply snatch the food they need. A slim woman may also be a status symbol. They would always snatch food for her, while the women of the defeated had to store energy in happy times for the years of famine. Maybe the Venus of Willendorf is the Goddess of some peaceful hungry hunters. Here we'll give the explanation for one of the major mysteries what women want in men. Why do women prefer bad guys?

If we take into account everything we've noted in the book so far, the explanation is simple. Since people, either as a species, a nation, or as individuals in their lives, have been getting into situations such as the shipwreck dilemma, or some resource crisis, the genes of those women, who have been choosing men that were acting adequately in those circumstances, have survived, and those were the bad guys who were willing to cheat, lie, rob, kill etc.. Women who chose good guys were less likely to pass through that narrow bottleneck of evolution.Thanks to recessive genes and other genes, which aren't activated in every generation, in normal times, society has been establishing its stability by activating genes that encourage "good" behavior that enables cooperation between people.

That can also explain masochism as a trait of many women who choose men who abuse them. If those women didn't enjoy being abused, they couldn't stand bad guys and they wouldn't have sexual intercourses with them. Thus we can see again that nature itself is evil and that it doesn't reward good guys and women, but men with sadistic tendencies and women with less or more masochistic tendencies. Those are functionally ideal types, and of course there are masochistic men and sadistic women.

The specialization reflected in the results of the solved IQ tests, which contain various types of tasks is of great importance, when it comes to specialization. It's clearly only one type of intelligence, but still the one that all abilities depend on. IQ could be compared to the power of a computer processor, while other types could be compared to the quality of other computer components, such as a graphics card, for example. An extremely high IQ makes someone successful in various fields, but it doesn't mean that he's necessarily musically gifted, wise, etc. As we've seen, the basic types of intelligence are male and female. The male intelligence is specialized in the knowledge of nature, while the female intelligence is specialized in the knowledge of social relations, i.e. the knowledge of power relations.

Classical IQ tests show the ability to solve certain tasks that are mostly related to the g factor, which is a useful and very reliable psychometric construct. Modern tests are culturally very refined so that education, general knowledge or belonging to a particular civilization has almost no role in the ability to solve the tests.

According to those tests conducted in different cultures, there is a different distribution of intelligence quotients in male and female population. Women are mostly concentrated around the average with a small percentage of women who are well below average or well above average. On the other hand, a significant number of men are well below or above the average. How to explain that?

We've already noticed that the species risks through man and less or higher intelligence can sometimes turn out to be the solution for survival, depending on the natural conditions. More intelligent people are capable of solving various problems, but that intelligence may also indicate to them the risk of certain endeavors and then they can be inhibited by the fear. Good risk assessment, when the risk is extremely high, will adversely affect the man's determination to make the decisions that are sometimes essential. Also, we have to bear in mind that for a man, will is the basic trait that determines his manhood. We can see that will is more important trait in evolution than intelligence by the fact that women like that quality better in sexual selection. In such moments of high-risk, less intelligent men, who are less aware of danger are getting more popular. Therefore, their will is less inhibited. Although many will die, some will survive and thus prove themselves successful in natural selection. Due to the function of man as a risk factor, natural selection has enabled those men who survived and who are successful to fertilize a large number of females and increase the distribution of their genes, which have been approved by nature, within the species. That trait of sexual behavior, when more women choose one man, can also lead to significant social problems that we'll discuss in the part dealing with liberal-aristocratic and patriarchal-democratic sexual morality.

First, we'll deal with male and female morality. Cognitive task of a man is harder and therefore the likelihood of one becoming successful thanks to only his or her decisions is quite impossible. Kant believed that in fact we can't know with certainty the consequences of our actions and that the evaluation of moral actions must be based on one's intentions. The intentions of moral agents make certain actions moral or immoral. Still, Kant has taken that to the other extreme. He wanted to defend the following principle. There are certain activities that are immoral no matter who does them or when. Amazed by Newton's universal validity of laws of nature, he wanted to apply in an unnatural and violent way the universality that's valid for nature to matters concerning society, i.e. morality. His *Categorical Imperative*, which we've already explained, is a form by which we test the validity of certain behavior rules in terms of being moral or not.We believe that this system doesn't give us real opportunities to treat a procedure as positively moral. Yet, it allows us to reject some that might serve the abusers of our freedom. Kant makes suggestions for actions that we can accept as positively valid and universally applicable to all intelligent beings in all situations, such as: "Don't lie" and "Don't make false promises". The latter basically comes down to the former.

To defend his thesis, as a response to the French philosopher Benjamin Constant Kant wrote a text entitled *On a Supposed Right to Lie from Philanthropy*. In that essay, Kant gives a creepy example of a boy in whose house a man being hunted by a hitman is hiding. The murderer comes across the house and he asks the boy if his prey may be hiding somewhere inside the house. Kant believes that the boy should tell the truth to the murderer because a lie is immoral regardless of circumstances. Kant argues that, as far as the boy knows, by then the hunted man could have already left the house. But that's irrelevant, since according to Kant, even if he knew that he would endanger innocent man's life, he should speak the truth.

I believe that from the above, every reader can draw his own conclusion about how defensible and acceptable Kant's position regarding lies is. The writer of this piece will present his suggestion for formal ethics that solves the problem of lying and other morally ambiguous actions and situations. The solution is as follows. The morality of certain actions that can be assessed as moral or immoral depends on the power of a certain moral agent. The term agent has been recently used in ethics to refer to the various types of entities that are moral agents. Thus, that term refers to both subjects and institutions that can act morally or immorally.

In formulating this formal ethics, we went from the idea that moral agents must fulfill one logical-ontological condition in order to be moral agents at all. That condition is mere existence. In order to act morally, a person must first exist. Existence assumes that there's some source of energy - for humans it's air, water, food, and first of all the space they occupy. Institutions also require people, space and finances. If he has the power to get all of that, we can see someone as a moral agent. It's totally different with someone who's without those basic life necessities. He doesn't really have a choice and therefore he doesn't have freedom which is a basic precondition for moral action. That already paves the way for us. Is lying an immoral act for someone who's trying to save his life, provide one of those necessities, preserve his freedom or dignity?

It's important, and crucial, that we don't connect the acting in the morally right way to the consequences that result from it. We don't disagree with Kant in that domain. The moral correctness of an action arises from the intentions and, we add - the power of a person who acts. We'll imply the intention and we'll stress the power. The same action, and we'll deal with lies and murder, is moral depending on the power of the person who does it.

In the first example, we'll deal with the case of gaining and losing freedom. Let's imagine a slave captured in a war who is also a child in the Iron Age, like Conan at the beginning of the movie. His guards take him to the mine where he'll probably spend the rest of his life working hard, without proper and sufficient nutrition, frequently tortured by guards who'll beat him without guilt and all of that will lead him to an early death, which may not be so terrible considering the life they intended for him. While children, who are easy to make obedient slaves, are taken by special guards, most of the army that participated in the conquest and enslavement goes away. Over time, since children are too slow, a part of the army consisted of guards, who are taking them, can't keep up so they make an agreement with the officers not to wait for them since they're too slow and they continue their journey at a slow pace determined by the physical limitations of children over hilly and mountainous terrain, covered by forest. The soldiers aren't worried as they don't expect any enemy, and one day, having climbed the hill, which dominates that area, they notice a path that would serve as a shortcut. However, since they haven't been familiar with the area, they lack courage to take a trip through an unknown territory. Having heard their conversation, our hero, a young boy who doesn't accept his fate, decides to interfere. The boy knows that the shortcut goes through the territory of a wild, but to enslaved children friendlier tribe, which would certainly quickly notice the intruders and prepare an ambush for them and the subsequent chaos might change the dark fate. Pretending to be interested in better treatment by guards in exchange for information, the boy tells them that he knows the way well and that he'll be happy to be the guide in exchange for a place on the wagon and a piece of meat. Innately suspicious guards try to intimidate him with threats if he cheats them, and one of them slaps him, very hard for his age; the boy bursts into tears but still he remains determined in his intention of lying to them. Finally, to make sure that the boy won't trick them, one of the guards chains a boy to his wrist by a metal chain so that the boy can't escape if he deserves to be punished, as he has promised to him, by cutting his neck.

On the first night in an unknown territory, the guards are attacked and killed, mostly at sleep. The boy, our hero, has managed to be faster than the guard he's been chained to and he kills him with a knife which he's taken from his dead companion, while his personal guard has been fighting with one of the attackers, thus being prevented from punishing the child. After a short and sudden fight, the guards have been defeated and the children free.

As the example shows, the boy has lied and committed murder with the intention of freeing himself, and changing his sad fate. He couldn't use any other weapon except the lies and the "brutal murder" of his guard from the back, while he's been fighting with the attacker. Since the boy's been practically unable to get his freedom, he's resorted to lies that *aren't moral maxims* but *tools of the helpless*. As long as lies are used by the helpless to protect their lives, basic resources, freedom and dignity, no immorality can be attributed to them. Lie if you don't have other tool to protect your life and the lives of your loved ones, life resources, freedom and dignity - let it be our maxim of survival, but of course not morality. With Kant, there's a formal condition for the maxim to be universally acceptable for all intelligent beings. We'll introduce the condition for the maxim to be universally acceptable for all helpless intelligent beings. Strong people don't need lies to defend their goods, listed in the maxim of the helpless. That's why the lies of the powerful people are immoral. If there were some divine powerful being, who would use lies to accomplish his goals, it would be absolutely immoral.

We're also obliged to give an example for using lies in the situation of the powerful people. As an example of immorality, there's a historical example of colonialism when technologically, scientifically, militarily, and economically powerful Western European civilization used lies to take away the territory from the natives all around the world. The basic life resource - territory or space has been taken away from the natives using lies, false promises, and false contracts. The disrespect of the Kosovo Agreement in 1999 (UN resolution 1244), which was, by the way, imposed by force and which ended up in NATO's military intervention on Yugoslavia, has shown that the West continues with that practice. The immorality of the powerful stems from the options they have. While the weak don't have a choice and therefore they can't be moral agents, since the possibility of choice is necessary for freedom and freedom is an important assumption necessary for morality, the powerful always have other options. The powerful can simply afford to respect the agreements, especially those imposed by themselves.

To emphasize our point, we'll reevaluate all of Nietzsche's values. According to Nietzsche, there's the morality of the weak and the morality of the strong, and we'll stick to that, but we'll replace the formal conditions and the contents of those two moralities. For us, moral plebs will represent beings, who choose life at all costs, while moral aristocracy will choose death rather than the violation of previously accepted moral norms. In this part also, we'll agree with Kant that we have to accept moral norms a priori before experience shows us whether they benefit us or not. *Lie, snatch, trick someone, don't have compassion* - these are all contents that beings who wish to survive in this world in certain situations can use without being taken as immoral people. All the weak have the right to use these means of survival. First of all women and children, then slaves, proletarians, people without any land, the poor, the ugly, the inexperienced, the unemployed, etc. Just as the powerful have the right to stop them. That fight isn't a matter of morality.

We'll set the matters in the way that although the weak have the right to qualities that aren't traditionally seen as moral, they don't have the right to power. Only the strong can have the right to rule. Those who are able to carry out their intentions without lying and force, if such beings exist and theoretically it's quite possible; they're created to rule. Those who can afford the luxury of compassion and mercy are true aristocracy. Can we really see an aristocracy in Napoleon, who was full of complexes or in the unfortunate Borgias who were able to do everything for this world. Nietzsche has really stranded. For many people, this world simply isn't good enough to do anything to survive in it. This world isn't the best possible. It's often ugly, filled with illnesses, it makes many people frustrated and unhappy and some people have the right not to appreciate it. Just like Schopenhauer doesn't appreciate it, but he also rejects it at all costs, which we don't want to do. This world is tolerable to a certain extent and it possesses some beauty and joy, although it's obviously imperfect. We won't judge those who are ready to lie and kill to stay in it, but we admire those who don't want to consume it at all costs. Nor, like Nietzsche, can we judge anyone who believes that such a miserable world as ours isn't the only one that exists and that there must be something better.

There's the universal standard of morality, although there are two basic moralities- the morality of the strong and the morality of the weak, i.e. male and female morality, which isn't exclusively only that. The power that Nietzsche appreciates so much is the criterion we use to assess the same actions. In the case of the helpless, who are turned to life at all costs, it isn't immoral to lie and kill in situations like the shipwreck dilemma. When we have the power in this world which we can use to defend our interests without lying and killing, but still we do the opposite, then we're immoral beings. We have real power when we're detached from this world that allows us to act according to pre-established moral norms although it may harm us, or even possibly kill us. None of us can know for sure which one of these moral niches he belongs to, until life tests him.

To support our theory, we'll use a few more examples. We need to emphasize another good quality of our theory. In utilitarianism, the moral rightness of actions is attributed to the good produced by those actions. Assessing the correctness of one's actions according to their consequences is close to common sense. After all, law, apart from the intention, which legal science treat as an attempt, pays the most attention to the consequences of some actions. Thus, someone can commit a crime even though he didn't have the intention of doing it, such as involuntary manslaughter. Law generally defines certain actions as illegal, based on their outcomes. First and foremost, utilitarianism is a theory relating to institutions that have power, such as the government or parliament of a country. The idea behind utilitarianism is that such institutions are guided in their work by principles that will benefit as many people as possible. The word utilitarianism itself originates from the Latin adjective *utilis* meaning *useful*.

Our theory that connects morality to power is consistent with the intentions of utilitarianism, although it doesn't assess moral actions based on their consequences. Consistency stems from the fact that there's a correlation between power and having good and bad consequences. The powerful can easily do great harm and cause unfavorable consequences for society, while the weak can't.

For example, take some medium-sized company. A cleaning lady and the CEO can't have the same moral responsibility bearing in mind their level of power. Their lie to their colleagues can't be equilizied. The same lie doesn't bear the same moral responsibility. Imagine that a cleaning lady comes from a very poor family, with great problems to feed it. The cleaning lady decides to steal some hygiene products to reduce the expenses in the family budget and provide more financial means for food. That action is immoral, but it's a low level immorality. If the CEO steals the same amount of hygiene products, his action will be the action of high level immorality. Given his position and income, he has enough power and he doesn't have to do such things. Also, the CEO has much wider range of opportunities to commit immoral actions. If a cleaning lady lies about doing her job, for example she says that she's cleaned a room twice, and she's done it only once, it's again a low level immoral action (since her lack of power doesn't allow her to do more than that). On the other hand, if the CEO lies to shareholders about the success of the business, he commits a high level immoral act given his position. Both cases are immoral in terms of intention to deceive other people, and here we agree with Kant, but unlike him we see slight differences. According to Kant, you are either moral or immoral. If a boy in his example lies, although he's absolutely helpless, and by our criteria regarding power completely innocent; if he tries to lie to a murderer, according to Kant, he's as immoral as some powerful prince of an important country who lies over trivial things.

We believe that life isn't black and white. We can be more or less immoral. The immorality of moral agents and their acts results from their power. Connecting morality to power is correlated with the consequences that result from it. The fact that the cleaning lady has lied about cleaning the floor only once won't do any significant harm, but if the CEO misleads the shareholders by showing them false reports, then the entire company may collapse, leaving the shareholders without assets and the employees without jobs. The criterion regarding power fulfills the requirement of ethics for formalism, and more importantly it's in line with common sense.

We'll extend our example to emphasize the quality of our criterion. In the case when there's a risk of an infectious disease outbreak in some country, the power of a cleaning lady rises. Imagine that the spread of that contagious disease can easily be prevented by maintaining good hygiene in living space. The same act of not doing the job properly in a new power relation makes the cleaning lady immoral person of higher level.

Having exposed our morality theory which is related to power, we'll go back to the morality of men and women. Kant believed that women and peasants can't be moral beings. Is he right if we look at things from our point of view? First, we've looked at things from the ideal men and women's point of view of, then we've watered it down by acknowledging that most people aren't ideal types. However, although some genes that produce typically masculine or typically feminine traits can be found in both sexes, there's a concentration of genes that determine masculine traits in men and vice versa, genes that determine feminine traits are concentrated in women. (In fact there's a small number of genes which are particularly feminine or masculine. Most genes are general, and chromosomes determine which sex they'll adjust to.) The reason for this is the function within the species that each sex performs, and therefore it's more useful to use the ideal types for the explanation. There are women who prefer to choose men by their physical appearance. However, evolution doesn't encourage such behavior and such genes programmes aren't dominant in the female sex. It's interesting that even women in modern societies, who are financially independent, in the first place appreciate the success of a man, and only then his physical appearance. However, there's a tendency that with greater financial emancipation, women pay more attention to a man's appearance.

We'll note that women's preferences for successful men also depend on life experience. Attractive girls who come from poor areas will rather chase a successful man. The same goes for the experience related to age. With age, man's financial success becomes more important for girls than other factors. Man's social status becomes important earlier, so boys with more important status within a society are more attractive to girls. Clearly, that's related to the reasons given in our analysis of the hunter-gatherer society. The logic of discovery directs women to men that other men have already recognized. People used to have children very early. What modern society considers a bad thing, i.e. a minor pregnancy, hunter-gatherer communities considered normal. After all, in agricultural societies as well, couples strived to have children early. Unlike contemporary romantic ideas about love for children, our ancestors had children either for instincts or for future benefits. More children meant more warriors and manpower, and woman who wasn't able to give birth could be easily rejected. The development of agriculture has provided a sedentary lifestyle and a significant population increase, but it has also helped the development of patriarchal morality. We now use morality in a slightly different meaning, narrowing its scope to the regulation of sexual behavior.

In various species that live in a group, there's a division into alpha males and those that are pushed away from social events and live their lives on the outskirts. In African buffalo, weaker males are usually positioned on the outskirts of the herd and therefore they are more exposed to be attacked by predators. The similar is in baboons and many other species. In wild cats, weak males are completely expelled from the group, while in most species they have low sexual status. Also, in our close cousins chimpanzees, who are sexually relatively liberal, there's a hierarchy and alpha male must be first satisfied.

Therefore, the development of patriarchal morality in humans is quite strange because its goal is that each man and woman finds himself or herself a couple, preferably for life. We won't try to give some definitive answer on the genesis of patriarchal morality, but we'll note that there are three major types of sexual morality regarding human sexuality in history and those are: female morality, which we'll call liberal-aristocratic and two male moralities, which we'll call patriarchal-democratic and warrior-aristocratic morality. We'll name those two others moralities male since they aim to preserve a group, which is the characteristic of the male sex within the species. We'll show how liberal-aristocratic morality badly affects group cohesion and makes it vulnerable in the conflict with other groups, where men are the ones who choose women.

THE INVASION OF THE BARBARIANS

We must emphasize that we use the term morality primarily as a set of rules and customs that regulate relations among people, serve to overcome conflicts and bring stability to the group. We'll stress sexual relations since we believe they're crucial for the very existence of a society. Regarding sexuality, there's female and male morality, but male morality has its version for the weak and for strong. Aristocratic-liberal morality is when woman is entirely free to consume her sexual relations. First of all, that refers to freedom in choosing a partner. The term *aristocratic* itself means the best. It's natural that in sexually liberal societies, women want the best men.

Liberal-aristocratic, from now on - female morality has been already present in hunter-gatherer communities, and it appears again in urban culture as dominant. The name of the popular series about promiscuous women who make their own choices of men and they mostly choose men from high social class, i.e. they choose successful men, is indicative - Sex and the City. It's liberal since a woman doesn't have any barriers in terms of social norms when it comes to choosing a man. The influence of the society on her choice is minimal or nonexistent. It's contrary to patriarchal morality where parents, family in general and social norms determine or have a strong influence on the choice of sexual partner and the way they enter sexual relations. It's aristocratic because attractive women, who have the greatest number of options, tend to choose the most powerful men - the elite, even if society itself isn't aristocratic. Every society, even if it may not have an aristocratic norm of social behavior, has some leading "aristocracy" that can be very plebeian in its behavior.

So-called groupie girls are often occurrence in contemporary urban culture. Those girls are waiting in line to sleep with successful sportsmen for example footballers and basketball players, which doesn't differ from the Amazonian hunter-gatherer cultures where their groupie girls admire the best wrestlers in the village.[44]It's natural that woman wants the genes of the physically most powerful man. Contemporary groupie girls, including those who chase celebrities, i.e. the most popular men like rock and hip hop stars, are in the iron grip of their urges, which are determined by their genes. Those girls inherited a successful recipe for survival – to have sexual intercourses with the physically most powerful or the most popular men, because the latter have social influence and power. On the other hand, more intelligent women will have sexual intercourses with men who have direct influence on social opportunities such as politicians and successful businessmen.

In societies where female morality rules, women get the highest quality seed in a very simple way. The social norms themselves aren't dangerous for women at all. The only obstacles are presented by other women. Since the goal of some woman is a certain man, chosen by her cognitive powers, the main obstacle may be posed by another woman, who is interested in the same man. Sharing one man is counterproductive because in that case resources are divided into more parts. The best option for a woman is to have the whole man to herself. Traits of a female prey (man) have determined by natural selection what kind of women can survive evolution more easily than other women. Those are the women who hunt alone and keep their prey for themselves. The fact that women are often compared to domestic cats who are individual hunters isn't unusual, and even when they hunt in group, each of them hunts for herself.

---

[44]Helen Fischer, Um zene, p.303 Original in English "The First Sex"

Another interesting quality of a woman hunter is that when she already has one man for herself, she wants to catch another one too. Apart from getting additional resources, she can enjoy the hunt itself, uninhibited by the necessity of success. Such female morality has its advantages for the species but it also has one very negative feature, which is the destruction of cohesion of the male group.

The benefits of hunt and defense in a group, one of the most important traits of males of our species, can be seen in various other areas as well. The first and the most important on the list is warfare. If any man fought alone, he wouldn't have any success. So, it's logical then that he fights together with others. Since reason isn't sufficient to support the preservation of the group due to the conflicts of individual interests, evolution has left alive those men who carry genes that are at first sight irrational. People often react emotionally to various contents that serve to support the cohesion of a group such as anthem, flag, patriotic and fan songs etc. The way of speaking, dressing, characteristic colors, coats of arms, every symbol that denotes a group provokes, especially in young people, emotional fixations, which aren't always reasonable. Young people perceive a group as something that defines an individual's identity to such an extent that a person can't imagine his life without being a part of groups whose longevity often goes beyond his own life.

As an example of the detriment of developing our own individuality for warfare, we can take the modern US Marines, whose training contains the breaking of the personality that has had previously developed as individual personality. When an individual's ego is broken, it gets rebuilt accordingly to the interests and identity of the group. Marine is in the first place the part of the Marines community, and only then he's John Smith. That method is mainly successful with young people. The fact that men mature relatively late, averagely, at about the age of twenty-seven, and the fact that the average life expectancy in hunter-warrior cultures was barely more than thirty years, tells us that maturity wasn't useful for most men in their warrior careers. Ratio can reduce courage, which isn't good for a warrior. The best ones, who survived and left offspring, spent most of their lives thinking in the categories of belonging to a group. Only later, when they had a chance to become leaders due to their experience, they became mature. At that age, they probably had more children who survived due to the genes passed to them by those winners selected by nature. Of course, as alpha males they had a chance to have more children.

For all the above-mentioned reasons, to understand group in history and prehistory, we must turn to the traits of today's young people with an emphasis on teens and 20-year-olds. It's easy to notice that young men are easily organized into gangs and fan groups if the nation doesn't have a way of engaging them in a war.

Sociology has noticed that young people are more moral than older people. Young people are more willing to subordinate their interests to the common good, and the common good in history has been the good of its warrior group, tribe, and nation. Although it may seem strange that behavior contrary to selfish interest leaves people alive and enables further transfer of their genes, there's a simple explanation. Since people don't know with certainty the consequences of their actions, it can often happen that they live through some dangerous situations where they've wanted to sacrifice themselves for the group. Willingness to sacrifice strengthens group cohesion. It isn't unusual for young people that they want to be heroes, and the biggest part of every army has consisted precisely of young men. The behavior that conditions young people till their late twenties is the product of genes that were under intense pressure due to war demands and behavior that's in line with that demands. While rational selfish behavior can create enemies and prevent us from achieving our goals, selfless behavior and loyalty to the group make us acceptable to the people, who we are forced to cooperate with. Selfish behavior, which opposes the interests of a group, has been harshly punished within hunter - warrior groups, often by exile outside the community, which meant almost certain death.

Joined action brings so much benefit that genes, which generate social cooperation within one community, had to be positively selected. Interestingly, friendship is typical of male groups, which is contrary to female individualism. Friendship explains the psychological willingness to sacrifice oneself for another person. War veterans often mention that the reason why they fought in a certain situations wasn't because of some ideology or politics but because they didn't want to leave their comrades in arms in the lurch. The very etymology of the word friendship (camaraderie) indicates selflessness.[45] In women, camaraderie couldn't develop due to the type of prey they hunt. Men can divide hunt or war prey by certain acceptable standards, while women aren't capable of that.

Men's trait to organize themselves into groups brings benefits in every action, including the construction of irrigation systems that encouraged the creation of the first countries. The development of agriculture has led to the increased power of ordinary men. Man didn't have to be a successful hunter anymore and he could feed his family simply by working harder. That allowed for the occurrence of patriarchal morality. There wasn't any need for a female to mate predominantly with an alpha male. In fact, female liberal-aristocratic morality raises a serious problem in the male group functioning. Men who aren't the subject of women's selection may develop negative qualities for the survival of the group. It isn't just jealousy that comes first to mind. They can simply become demotivated. This isn't such a big problem in the conditions of hunter-gatherer communities, since they have to fight for bare survival. However, in the conditions of abundance brought by agriculture, the fact that most men aren't the first choice of some woman can ruin society. How will community be defended if most men feel that they actually don't have anything to defend?

---

[45] It's the case in Serbian language. The term for a friend (comrade) in Serbian is *drug* and it refers to another person (drugi) indicating selflessness.

It's natural that in response to that problem, patriarchal morality has been created with the tendency to pair one man and woman for life. In rural farming communities, that solution is relatively effective. The problem has arisen with the development of city centers. In urban economy, wealth is higher at the city level but tends to move from hand to hand. A trader, with trade being the city's main economic base, can easily fail due to the uncertainty of trade ventures. Since the needs of the economy in a big city, which is a trade center, remain great, another trader will easily replace him and then women's traits become prominent. While in the countryside, (we are talking about pre-modern times), there's generally low social mobility and a farmer can expect to spend his entire life being a farmer just as more than ninety percent of other men can expect the same, mobility is higher in the city due to dynamic economy and therefore it's easier to change places. In rural economy, there isn't sufficient room for women to show their hunting skills, mostly because of the lack of bigger prey and the stability of the available one. The opposite is true in city; women easily get into the situations similar to the one mentioned in the previous chapter to show why women aren't immoral, even though they leave a "beloved" man. That's one of the reasons why men get discouraged and men's groups lose cohesion.

Another, more important reason is that urban economy creates more wealth. That allows for larger women's economic independence from men. Thus, women want more successful men, but then there's a lack of them. A large number of men and women remain unmatched. Economic wealth also makes women more important in raising children, and allows them to raise children without man or with men who are submissive to women. Women create new generations of male individuals who aren't able to maintain group cohesion. Male children, raised mainly by women, lack true masculine archetypes they would look up to. All that leads to the decline in the quality of new male generations and their ability to organize themselves. In Etruria, which was conquered by Roman barbarians and in Crete[46] in the period before the conquerors from the mainland destroyed the urban civilization struck by a volcanic eruption on Santorini, in the religious-artistic presentations couples of male-female deities appeared where female deities dominated over immature male counterpart. That testifies to men's low status in urban cultures. In fact, men become so subordinate over time that the main male-female relationship between mother and son becomes incestuous. This is evidenced by the myths and religions arisen in cultures where women have been dominant. Aphrodite (Astarte, Ishtar, Kibela are just different names of the same material that refer to the great matriarchal goddess) is also associated with the Eastern myth that tells about her young lover – in fact, her son. In various versions, that young god castrated himself. The great mother wants him only for herself but he betrays her with a rival. She discovers and curses him, and the young god castrates himself due to regret, so that his manhood wouldn't serve anyone but his mother. That would be a society dominated by women. The woman's partner is irrelevant, and all attention is paid to the son who loses his main male symbol - his genitals. Obviously, such a civilization becomes a futile Freudian case unable to cope in the world and becomes the prey of male barbaric (although often few) warrior groups. The fight between masculine and feminine principles in the second millennium AD has intensified so much that a sinless conception, or birth, occurs in Greece. Athena, the goddess of wisdom, was born from the Zeus' head and not from the uterus. In the other end of the Mediterranean basin, the Jewish god is the creator of the *ex nihilo*

---

[46] There aren't any significant archeological findings from the Paleolithic in Crete and other eastern Mediterranean islands. The absence or extinction of a warrior-hunter community explains how the Cretan civilization developed as a case where women were in absolute authority. Crete was a fully civil society under the authority of women and naturally - it was won by male warriors. It's interesting to compare this case with strengthening of the position of women in Europe and moving towards civil society. Heroes aren't popular. Europe will probably experience the fate of Crete if it continues that way.

world. He doesn't need substance– something that's fundamentally feminine; he actually creates substance without any participation of woman.

Women's independence leads to a process that's one of the main causes of ancient civilizations collapse. Ordinary men, including the elite, believing that their women have been corrupted, look for women from regions where patriarchal upbringing is still strong. The fathers of those women from patriarchal areas naturally tend to give their daughters to wealthy men from city. Over time, with the spread of urban influences from the center to the outskirts, migrations of rural population occur, mainly women. They themselves seek to approach the center of civilization by searching more powerful men and freedom from patriarchal chains. The outskirts of civilization influenced by the city center remain almost completely without women. The metropolitan area acts like a black hole sucking in women. That urban civilization influence can be felt hundreds, even thousands miles away from the center. All that place men on the outskirts of these events in a Hamlet's dilemma. Should they accept to die out slowly or should they resort to weapons? It's interesting that the marginal men in the areas where the agricultural value ceases take women from the hunter-gatherer communities, since the possibility of having food is greater so they are more attractive to them. Hunter-gatherers in the prehistory and history were the last men in this order of causality. Faced with the choice between extermination and the war for women, they naturally used their hunter -warfare skills to enslave less war prone farmers, who were less skillful in war. The traits of an aristocracy, which imposed itself by force as the ruling elite in ancient times and times before that, support well that hypothesis. The inclination towards hunting as a major sport shows the origins of ancient and medieval aristocratic communities. Over time, those groups of warrior aristocracy, having realized that not even the elite of the city center can defeat them, attack the centers of urban civilizations.

To begin with, we'll illustrate that hypothesis with a few historical events, by giving the example of Mesopotamia. The original barbarians, who conquered the Mesopotamian cities, came from the Zagros Mountains, and it's quite certain that women didn't have any dilemma between the difficult mountain life and the comfortable, urban one in the developed plain. As an illustration of that, we'll take an example from epic literature that certainly preserves the memory of similar historical processes. It's the poem *The Marriage of King Vukasin,* where King Vukasin comes to the wife of the mountain duke Momcilo, who's undoubtedly poorer and accustomed to a difficult life, which his wife doesn't wish, so she betrays him because of the promise of a rich king from the plain. It's quite certain that this poem preserves the memory of the older events that preceded the time of King Vukasin and Duke Momcilo. Since it's one of the oldest poems in Serbian epic poetry, it's definitely an event from a distant past or there's also a possibility that it never happened in the Balkans.

We won't stick to a chronological order in presenting our examples, so we'll give the famous story about the rape of the Sabine women as the next example. What's striking in this case is the fact that the plot is related to the first Romans in the suburban areas of the Etruscan civilization. We could see from Greek and Roman historical sources that they believed that the Etruscans allowed their wives too much. The Romans conquered the Etruscan civilization, which was much more developed but divided and corrupted by comfort. Draw your own conclusions, bearing in mind that we can conclude from Roman myths that the period of early Rome, including the republic, was strongly influenced by male morality, with many examples where a person sacrificed his own interests for the common good and other stories that are educational for a warrior culture.

What about the Trojan War describing an event where the wife of Spartan king has acted the same like the wife of Duke Momcilo? She decides to betray her husband because of the richer man. There's the process we described behind the entire Trojan

War poem. Troy, due to its geographical location, becomes a prosperous urban civilization that begins to attract women from all over the region. The poor Greek ancestors, to prevent the Trojans from taking their best women, choose a war as a solution. Helen of Troy from Greek mythology is just a symbol of all the attractive women who chose the Trojans over the Greeks.

There are probably similar processes behind the settlement of Greeks to modern Greece, previously inhabited by the famous Pelasgians[47]. It's certain that farmers who migrated from Asia Minor spread their agricultural values until they threatened, through the process we've described, some tribes that were more hunting and war oriented, and less oriented towards agriculture and trade. Those tribes turned to conquest until they became a ruling aristocracy. It's quite possible that this was an even broader process that threatened the ancestors of the Aryans, who we already mentioned. They reacted to the influences of the Middle East and India urban civilizations, where agriculture spread from Elam, a Middle Eastern agricultural state, by creating a distinctly warlike culture that over time destroyed some of the city centers responsible for those processes such as Mohenjo - Daro and Harappa.

Patriarchal-democratic morality is a natural sexual morality of the defeated groups because it provides women for male losers. It was named after the Latin name for father, i.e. the head of the family - *pater familias*. He has the final word when it comes to managing the whole family, which is often an agricultural community or even a warrior group, but subordinated to aristocrats. Patriarchal morality can be successfully integrated with aristocratic morality, creating nations and it's relatively stable. The main danger to patriarchal morality is urban culture prevalence. Although more significant, city was throughout large part of human history quantitatively in the shadow of village, the only place where patriarchal morality can be preserved.

---

[47] Members of the Neolithic matrilineal civilization

The development of cities in history had counterproductive results for cities themselves. Rome has sucked in its province, in a similar process that we've described. Roman historians lament that every generation of Romans is increasingly corrupt and less concerned about the general interest. Over time, native Romans were increasingly avoiding military duty so they were replaced by people from less civilized provinces. In times of empire, emperors often came from the Balkans because the army was largely Illyrian in origin. Thus, the present territory of Serbia gave a quarter of all Roman emperors. Just to mention Probus and Constantine.

While Rome managed to conquer new territories, in fact, while it was a dominant war oriented society, those processes couldn't harm it much. When Rome faced the unprofitability of its conquests, with the Parthians and Barbarians, who had excellent warfare skills, taking too much of Rome's resources and the barbaric countries couldn't contribute to large profit other than human resources, the processes became more noticeable. Entire nations were entering the territory of the empire. Finally, the most vulnerable men - the Huns - appeared as the main threat to Rome. Since Rome barely managed to defend itself, it could no longer maintain a strong army. Warrior morality, the general interest of the group, no longer resided in Rome. Various warrior groups occupied parts of the Roman Empire, converting agricultural and trade population into their subjects. The Goths, the Vandals and the Franks became new aristocracy. Barbarians are omnipotent sovereigns who contribute to social cohesion torn by female morality. A barbarian is a historically real Hobbesian Leviathan.

Similar processes that destroy the cohesion of a group occurred in Byzantium as well. More economically developed eastern part of the Roman Empire, which had the well-established capital in the best trading places of all time, which wasn't far from Troy, lasted longer. However, the Barbarians conquered Byzantium too. New barbarians kept coming to the territory of Byzantium, and Byzantium managed to convert them into its subjects, often with the help of Christianity. Thus, the Serbs and the Bulgarians integrated into the Byzantine commonwealth over time. However, at the same time, some new, more dangerous barbarians appeared in the east contemporary with the Slavic invasion (7th century). The Arabs were dangerous since they were religiously indoctrinated by the initiator of the entire Arab association - Muhammad.[48] This founder of religion succeeded in converting a primitive society on the outskirts of civilization into a warrior society that conquered that civilization. Their religion prevented them from becoming Byzantium-influenced Christians over time. However, civilization as the protector of female morality has diminished the power of these barbarians, so they became the prey of subsequent Turkish barbarians, who embraced Islam and became to some extent tolerable masters of the Arabs.

In the struggle for the throne of the remains of the Byzantine in the second half of 14th century, one of the pretenders drafted Turkish mercenaries into the war, encouraging them to conquer those remaining territories. Over time, Byzantine urban culture prevented the Byzantines from gathering sufficient

---

[48] The example of the Arabs from the period of Mohammed is seemingly counter example to our theory. These are the Barbarians who had too many women. The Arabs often fought among themselves during Muhammad's youth. The high mortality of men caused poor Arab tribes to kill female children at birth to maintain balance. Muhammad abolished infanticide, and the custom that a man could marry more women was intended to save widows and female babies from a dark fate. The reason may be because the Arabs, in relation to the period of Mohammed, have relatively recently transitioned from matrilineal to patriarchal society. The patriarchal society has been successful to certain extent in defending itself from the influence of civilization. At that period, Muhammad was the answer of the masculine principle to the influence of Byzantium and Persia's civilization. When Mecca became a trade center, the patriarchal tribal system was mortally threatened, and trade elite, which had increasing influence, began to emerge among the Arabs. At the very beginning, Muhammad destroys the potential return to a society of dominant female morality and transforms the Arabs into conquerors of civilization, which by its influence undermines the dominance of patriarchal morality in Muhammad's environment.

numbers of soldiers, leaving war to foreign mercenaries, who eventually conquered Byzantium. The Turks developed a form of culture where all were subordinate to one man - the Sultan. He's a male with a harem, like our distant relatives - gorillas. The Ottoman aristocracy didn't even exist in the European sense of the word since it was too dependent on Sultan. All power was concentrated in one place. Ottoman history has hardly had any periods of weakening central government. Civil wars took place within the family. All that caused patriarchal morality to become dominant for most ethnic Turks. It's helped them to preserve to this day as a group where the previously described processes have started to take place only in recent years.

An interesting example is China as well, which has been an agricultural civilization with many peasants, but also significant urban centers for a long time in history. The same processes we described allowed the emergence of barbarians (the Mongols) who conquered China and established themselves as their aristocracy. Ordinary Chinese people managed to save themselves from disappearance thanks to patriarchal morality itself.

In Europe, warrior groups and nations created the first medieval states. The aristocratic-warrior spirit of those elites was persevered until the Industrial Revolution, and even longer. The constant competition and war between the countries has encouraged the development of technological innovation and critical thinking, which helped European education make incredible progress in mastering nature and conquering large part of the world. To be honest, we must also admit that the development of capitalism in Western Europe, which is also a competitive activity that encourages male associations, has great merits too. Thus, traders have been joining to fund major research ventures. Yet, although trade and war may initially support each other since war requests finances, over time the aristocratic warrior culture disappears. After all, reasonable women will rather raise their children as traders than warriors.

In the long run, trade-urban culture destroys masculine values and warrior groups disappear. Today's Europe is engulfed in these processes and it's only a matter of time when the European democracies will be replaced by new countries that will emerge as result of the subjugation of a pacific European civilization by a small number of war-oriented groups.

***

This book first (Serbian) edition was written in 2010. Now (2019) we can conclude that Europe is to the great extent on the path of subjugation, perhaps even the disappearance of the native population, but this time it's more due to infiltration than conquest by the barbarians. Interestingly, women and feminist organizations play an important role in this process of diminishing European civilization. The existence of Sweden's first feminist government corresponds with the collapse of the Swedish nation and the Swedish man.

THE CONCLUSION - TROY WITHOUT HECTOR

The movie *Conan the Barbarian* is one of the finest works of the seventh art. In our book, we've been mainly explaining the philosophical ideas and problems that have been dealt with in this film. This work is mostly based on Nietzsche's philosophy, but as we've shown, there's a deviation from Nietzsche's philosophical heritage by creating more humane "overman" with the help of the artistic means available to film art. Also, Milius introduces the existence of the other world where a man's soul outlives the death of his body, manifesting it with the appearance of Conan's sweetheart, who saves his life in the fight with Rexor. Nietzsche despises the idea of another world.

However, deviation from Nietzsche's philosophy isn't essential because *Conan the Barbarian* positively portrays the philosophy of war and courage. Will, which is a main masculine trait and the foundation of Nietzsche's philosophy, is artistically displayed in a superb way. We can't remember any portrayal in art that presents the power of will better than the wheel of pain scene.

Schopenhauer's philosophy as well, which represents core of religions like Christianity and Buddhism, has its place in the movie. Will is also a central motive in Schopenhauer, to whom young Nietzsche looked up to. Schopenhauer believes that will needs to be eliminated and that anti-life concept is negatively portrayed in the movie. Nietzsche's and Schopenhauer's philosophies were deliberately the theme of the film. Regarding

Hegel's idea of a "struggle for recognition", we aren't sure whether Milius deliberately dealt with it or whether he came up with such a concept in some philosophically more undeveloped form. As we've already mentioned in the book, Milius's work contains many other philosophical ideas and problems of the soul that the director solves using artistic means. It's also striking that Milius has used his knowledge of history and archeology very skillfully to evoke the Iron Age atmosphere. The atmosphere created by this artist is more beautiful and true than that in most films dealing with real historical figures and events. We mustn't forget the partner in the script writing - Oliver Stone. The music of Basil Poledouris, which can be only compared in its epic power and beauty to Wagner's oeuvre, has a special place in the movie too. It's also worth mentioning the fantastic James Earl Jones, who represents one of the pillars of the movie, since it's hard to imagine a successful work of art without a convincing villain. The convincing villain is precisely what's missing in the sequel besides the other already mentioned shortcomings.

Arnold Schwarzenegger is a sine qua non. There was a desire to create a movie version of Conan the Barbarian for a long time, but it wasn't possible without an actor like Schwarzenegger. Only the muscular barbaric appearance of that artist allowed the creation of film. We believe that Schwarzenegger's acting is a perfect match to a high quality of the entire movie. Or maybe he hasn't been acting at all?

In our analysis of the film, we've followed the facts that can be rationally explained and conceptually presented. However, every work of art has some rationally inexplicable dimension. *Conan the Barbarian*, above all else, has that inexplicable beauty. Although this movie is the most philosophical movie, filmed so far, its true value lies in the inexplicable way in which it has managed to present those ideas to us.

This book has another dimension that relies on the ideas that are addressed in the film, but also has its independent life. In that parallel dimension, both ethics and the law applied to history are processed, allowing history to step into the field of the serious sciences. That law explains the appearance of historical barbarians.

In the part of the book dealing with ethics, we've discussed Kant's ethics and Nietzsche's dualistic moral, which is opposing to Kant's moral universalism. We've tried, by taking the most vital facts from those two opposing ethical positions, to make one synthesis that's in line with common sense. We've borrowed the idea of formalism and universal standards from Kant, while from Nietzsche we've borrowed the idea that there can't be morals that can be applied to all people and the knowledge that there are those who have power and the others who don't have it or they don't have it sufficiently. There's universality in the category of power, because every intelligent being can theoretically be in the position of having greater power or losing the existing one, which makes him more or less a responsible moral agent. We hold to formalism because we believe that morality depends on the position of power independently of any particular contents of morality. Unlike Kant, who believes that certain moral actions must be right or wrong for any being, basically independently of context, we assess actions according to the power of the moral agent in a given situation. The freedom that allows us our actions depends on power. More freedom requires more moral responsibility and vice versa. Unlike Kant's digital morality, where a person is either moral or not depending on his action in a certain case, we're introducing an analog morality that binds our responsibility to the level of freedom we have, depending on the power we have available. In Kant's famous example with a boy and a murderer, a boy can't be morally responsible for lying since it's his tool to fight the villain. Since a boy, who's weaker than a murderer has incomparably less power, his moral responsibility is reduced too. It's quite another matter if the killer, who at that moment has the power over life and death of his victims, uses a lie to find out where his prey is hiding. Suppose he makes a false promise that he'll spare a man who's hiding if he surrenders himself, while actually he intends to kill him. It's obvious that the killer would be completely immoral from our point of view.

We believe that our ethical concept is far more acceptable than Kant's and that it's close to common sense. It's also compatible with utilitarianism. This theory of rational decision making takes into account the consequences of our actions. It's clear that the decisions of the powerful people can have more serious consequences than those made by the people who are at low level in power hierarchy. Of course, we too, like Kant, firstly assess intentions, not consequences. Regarding evil intentions, there's a principled equality between powerful and powerless people. However, evil intentions of the powerless can be largely caused by their difficult life situation, so in most cases their responsibility is reduced at the level of intentions. On the other hand, powerful people are less frustrated in their lives, so their evil intentions are less justified and accordingly exposed to more severe moral criticism.

As for moral imperatives, they can be applied only to the elite. "Do not steal!" has its absolute meaning only for people at high level in the power hierarchy. A minister with a decent legal income, who still chooses to steal, commits the act of severe immorality. A person at the social bottom should take that moral imperative of the elite as a moral recommendation, which helps him to make a small, but given the situation, a significant contribution to maintaining the normal functioning of the community.

Also, there are some life circumstances outside of common morality, and that's an area where we're close to immorality. We've discussed the shipwreck dilemma as a problematic example. There're some situations when we can't make the right moral decision and survive or leave offspring. In such situations, only persons who are able to accept the complete rejection of the world, i.e. suicide, can act morally. By justifying suicide in certain situations, we oppose Kant but also Christian and public morals of most contemporary societies. In such cases, suicides have absolute power since they don't need anything from this world. Therefore, in such situations, they can act absolutely morally.

We need to explain what we consider absolutely immoral. An absolutely immoral situation is when we intentionally, without any particular need, create conditions for other people to lose their power to act freely and when they will be forced to act immorally. If we put people in a prison camp without any food, we would act absolutely immorally.

There's also the problem of supererogation, i.e. heroism in morality. Why do some people risk their lives for others? That can be explained by evolutionary reasons except in the case of suicides, who don't have offspring. In doing so, we must make a difference between male and female reasons. It's clear that a mother, who sacrifices herself for her children, increases the chances for her children to survive, thus transferring the gene of sacrifice to the species. Regarding men's reasons for sacrifice, the explanation is somewhat more complex. Since man gets his power from a male group, the sacrifice that will enable the group to survive or gain greater power is evolutionarily justified. Some situations in war look like suicide and yet some people survive. The tendency to take risks and gamble with one's life, which is much more common in male population, has its evolutionary basis. Although many who risk their lives will die, some will survive and transfer their genes further. Men's sexual function within a species is such that few men can maintain reproduction. That isn't the case with women. An individual woman is a bigger loss for the species than an individual man when considering only quantity. It's normal that women are generally more conservative and more cautious than men. Evolution hasn't been rewarding risky female behavior. It's necessary to save the largest number of women due to their biological function of reproduction. In the case of some disaster, the species will reproduce faster if there's a small number of men who survived and a larger number of women than if there's a large number of men who survived and few women. That's the case when it comes to the number of individuals. The situation is completely different when it comes to quality. New, successful genes, approved by nature's powers, are transferred more easily and quickly through a man who has useful mutation, even if the mutation initially manifested in a woman, his mother for example. Regarding transfer of quality, man is more important for the species.

Due to limited resources, it's natural that there will always be conflicts between people. Men will join groups to fight other men because if they fight individually, as in the Hobbesian example, they can always be defeated by those who joined groups. Eternal peace is just an illusion. The situation would be different if everything depended on humans but natural laws are such that they constantly act restrictively and select "evil" genes and "cultures". The world itself is far from being perfect; thus, the people who depend on it can't be much better. The only true morality that can exist is the one related to the interest of an individual men's organization. Some universal morality that can be applied to all can exist only in the conditions of high energy levels. Already with the first crisis, such morality becomes unsustainable for those who want to survive and leave offspring. Therefore, it can't be universal anymore because: 1) It can't be applied to all life situations; 2) It isn't the same for all intelligent beings. Those who wish to survive and leave posterity can't have the luxury of being moral like ascetics and suicides. When facing the severe lack of resources that isn't even sufficient to support the basic group of two individuals, we find ourselves in the situation outside of common morality, which prevents us to judge morally. Only suicides can act morally in such situations, since they have absolute power.

The fact that small boys from early childhood are generally interested in guns and play war related games while small girls take care about their dolls, tells us more about history and prehistory than any written documents or archeological sites. That fact the best testifies to biological functionalism within the species and the way to address resource scarcity issues. We believe that various energy crises are immanent to the world as such and that the above-mentioned fact proves our thesis. Noble human aspirations to solve problems peacefully are doomed to failure in certain, inevitable situations. Nowadays, "rational problem solving" means overcoming difficulties peacefully. With the knowledge, which we have nowadays, we can conclude that reasonable problem solving sometimes means conflict and war.

It's then natural to maintain the morality of war and courage within the male part of the species. History and archeology testify to that. There's a tendency in history for the development of urban civilization, which is destroyed or conquered by the barbarians at one point. Why does it happen? As we've already mentioned in the chapter dealing with the invasion of barbarians, women's economic and sexual emancipation that occurs in civilized societies in many ways undermines civilization's ability to defend itself. Moreover, civilization itself creates the conditions for the appearance of barbarians who will attack it. An economically emancipated woman doesn't need a man as a supplier anymore. On the other hand, a highly developed civilization gives freedom to women from a security point of view so they no longer need a man as a protector. For a woman, a man becomes a bit more than a bee that pollinates a flower. With the exception of a small group of men[49] who constitute, above all, the economic elite of the city and the urban civilization, most men aren't desirable enough to find a woman or keep her for a long time. That's why men incline to women from the outskirts of civilization who want to change the environment and reach relatively comfortable urban or metropolitan life. These processes lead to the shortage of women on the outskirts of civilization and their excess in the center.

Emancipated women teach their children that war is difficult, dangerous, bad and immoral. For those reasons, a large

---

[49]In the case of Crete in theMinoan period, even a small elite of men wasn't needed. Women performed all major functions, including ruling and priestly duties. A civil, non-heroic society doomed to failure.

percentage of urban children detest soldiers' duties and war as such. Urban civilizations increasingly fill vacant military ranks with children from the outskirts. This can be seen in the example of Rome. Initially, the Romans were barbarians on the outskirts of Etruscan civilization who had to take away women. Then, they established a warrior-aristocratic morality where woman was respected as the pillar of a family, at least with patricians. Probably the plebs expressed a classic patriarchal morality. In the period of the Late Republic and the Empire, women were increasingly emancipated and the military elite increasingly filled their ranks with Roman citizens from the province. At the time when recruiting in the Balkans was intensified due to the lack of native Roman soldiers, emperors were often from the Balkans too.

Emancipation of women leads to demographic problems as well. While in warrior cultures due to constant losses, more children need to be born and there's a social pressure to do so, in an urban civilization, a woman can give birth to only one child to calm her maternal instinct. In that way the population decreases over time. At the very beginning of the rise of civilization, when wars were rare and mostly on the outskirts, when medical care was improving along with hygiene and with the raise of amount of food, birth rate increased too. Patriarchal patterns were still strong. Over time, with the growth of women's emancipation, the birth rate has been decreasing. Metropolis has filled with people from the outskirts and the outskirts have emptied - a certain sign of civilization's collapse. Thus came the Barbarians, people accustomed to hard life, who firstly joined to plunder and then conquer the civilization. They were often warrior groups with a small percentage of women and their main goal was to take away women from civilized men. Of course, civilized men, aware that emancipated women didn't really belong to them, and softened by the luxury of civilization, were unable to offer adequate resistance. Having believed that money can buy everything, they were hiring mercenaries, i.e. other barbarians who were often turning against them. Those processes have taken place both in the east and in the west i.e. universally in human species. There's a pattern that repeats itself - Troy, Harappa, Babylon, China, Rome, Byzantium ... There's a law in history.

Those processes have been described in Serbian epic folk literature as well. In the poem Ailing Dojchin, the poet deals with the motive of the first man - to use the Hegelian expression-*barbarian,* who manifests his superiority over civil society with his sexual superiority. Citizens are forced to give him their wives since they're afraid to oppose him. Civil society is portrayed as fully atomized. The only man who opposes the barbarian is the representative of the old warrior aristocracy, which is dying out, after which the song is named. Although the poem deals with Thessaloniki, it's probably much older poem (like many other poems in Serbian epic literature) which uses more modern places and characters for a medieval and early modern period listener. In reality, over time urban civilization destroys the ability to raise someone like Hector who'll try to defend it.

At the heart of it all is the conflict between the functions of man and woman. For many men, it's valid to fight in a war, while from a woman's point of view it's important to save children. In civilizations, there's a tendency that long-lasting peace (Rome hasn't been directly threatened for centuries) leads to women's emancipation to the point where her natural and positive function has a negative impact on society. The wellbeing of children becomes far more important for women than general interest, which is basically men's moral idea. Society is being atomized, the old moral patterns of the male group are diminishing, the birth rate decreases, the population is maintained or increased by mechanical population growth. When those processes occur in provinces, civilization collapses. Barbarians, who are either destroying civilization or establishing themselves as protection elite, appear. It's interesting that at the same time when this conclusion was being written[50], RTS[51] channel was broadcasting a

---

[50] October – November 2010.
[51] Radio Television of Serbia, public service TV

report about the archeological site in Plocnik, a place in the south of Serbia. There were found the remains of the urban civilization that was the first one that was using metal in Europe, possibly independently of the Middle East. The figurines found at that site show women with short skirts, bare bellies and jewelry, which testifies to the great sexual emancipation of woman. As you may assume, according to the law of nature discussed in this book, civilization ended up by being destroyed by barbarians.

Translated by Mirjana Maric.

The afterword to the English edition of the book

Since there's a nine years difference between Serbian and English edition of the book, I wanted to make a few notes.

First of all, the reason I decided to publish it in English is because English is the modern lingua franca and the book isn't intended only for English native speakers. The book has been a success mainly with educated people in Serbia with a broad general knowledge. I remember how proud I was when my book was published and when I saw it in the window of an elite bookstore in the very center of Belgrade (Beogradski Izlog[52]) among the titles they recommended. Unfortunately, since I didn't have the patience for long negotiations with large publishers (one of them was interested but it was dragging out for a long time) and I had the urge, described in the introduction, to publish it as soon as possible. I decided on a small publisher that didn't have the strength for a serious marketing campaign so the project couldn't be finished properly. However, many people liked the book a lot, and one of the most respected university professors of sociology in Serbia told me that the idea of male-female relationships in urban centers as the cause of barbaric invasions was really original and that he would cite it in his future works. However, he reminded me that mono-causal causes in social processes are rare. The conclusion of the book was published on a reputable portal on politics and political theory in Serbia - NSPM[53], edited by one of my professors.

---

[52] The name of the bookstore

[53] Nova srpska politicka misao – New Serbian Political Thought

In the first months after the book was published, I was so occupied by the sequence of events in my personal life that I couldn't continue writing another book or to promote the existing one. The English edition is mostly the consequence of my readers' encouragement and their desire to recommend it to their friends abroad.

Secondly, I must mention that the English edition differs in details from the Serbian edition, but the essence is unchanged.

Regarding the paranormal event described in the introduction, when I think about it now, perhaps the best explanation is related to Hegel's philosophy. It's as if the world spirit, continuing its development and self-understanding, used my personal passions, preferences and the fact that I grew up in very specific circumstances of the collapse of a complex state, wars, the most severe economic sanctions imposed to some country, NATO bombing etc. to reach another level of self-realization. This time, when it comes to understanding of our own divisions into masculine and feminine principles and the potential destruction of civilizational advances that misunderstanding between genders has brought.

I have to conclude with great sadness that the West, which is the former champion of free speech and it's becoming a bastion of censorship, also makes me feel uneasy regarding the reception of my book in terms of political correctness.

Below, I wanted to mention a few things, related to the book itself. Firstly, I've given many examples from Serbian history and culture, but I hope it won't bother a foreign reader. I believe it's normal to try a national dish in a national cuisine restaurant. Thus, you can expect from a Serbian writer to write about examples from Serbian heritage. I should perhaps add the following regarding that. Based on the example of Prince Marko, one can't conclude enough about this extremely important character for Serbian culture, and I have the impression that I committed a sin when I presented him as a violent man.

Prince Marko was a historical figure and the last ruler in the Mrnjavcevic family. After the Serbian defeat on Marica and the death of his father Vukasin, King Marko inherited the throne of feudal territory on the territory of the present Republic of North Macedonia. He didn't have a choice and he became an Ottoman vassal, with the commitment that the country will be inherited by the Sultan after his death. Although there were more famous and powerful rulers and heroes, the character of King Marko became the most popular character of Serbian epic poetry. Perhaps the reason for that was because he stayed with his people and he advocated for the rights of Serbs and Christians under Ottoman rule, at a time when other feudal lords were running before Turkish conquests or converting to Islam, thinking only of themselves. After the collapse of the Serbian Empire and the war among the important lords for leadership, ordinary people suffered the most, especially after the Ottoman expansion in the Balkans. Although he's portrayed in epic poetry as the Sultan's vassal, quarreler and debauchee, the epic poet also gave him some very high ethical qualities, which served as an ideal to ordinary people. In the poem *Uros and Mrnjavcevic*, Marko rejects the offers of his father and uncles, who offer him a ruler's position in exchange for false testimony and he tells the truth even though it will only do him harm and a curse will be put on him. In the poem *Prince Marko removes the marriage tax*, he removes the marriage tax, and he kills a foreign landlord who introduced the right to the first wedding night in Kosovo for the poor who can't pay their *marriage tax*. Not to mention the poem *Prince Marko and Musa Kesedzija*, which we mentioned in the chapter dealing with "overman", where Marko regretted killing the better than himself.

All in all, during the Ottoman occupation, Prince Marko represented the Serbian people. Occupied, but not crushed in spirit. Combative and successful in battle, but after the loss of the country, often in the service of others. Serbian soldiers and nobles who didn't want to serve the Sultan, the ruler of another religion, mostly went to Hungary and later to Poland. Hussars were some type of light cavalry developed by the Serbs in the fight against the Turks and later adopted by other European armies. Thus, both in poems and in real life, Marko remained Turkish vassal. Historically, Marko died in the battle against the Wallachian Duke Mircea as Sultan's vassal, and allegedly, before the battle, he wished the Christians to win, even if he was the first to die. In the myth, Marko has lived for centuries and although he's been presented as a normal person with ordinary human flaws and virtues, he got the dimension of the ethical ideal for the Serbian people. Marko was also a popular mythic hero in neighboring peoples, especially Bulgarians.

I have to say that although I was growing up (actually I was a teenager) during the war for Yugoslav heritage and I consider myself a Serbian patriot, I don't cultivate any hatred in my heart towards other peoples of the former Yugoslavia. I'm sorry that the war happened in the first place, and I'm sorry that the co-causes of the war in the Western media are presented unilaterally and in a black and white way. The war had complex external and internal causes, about which I could write extensively. Even though the Western media and Western governments have waged the war against my people and country, I don't hate Westerners either. I'm aware that the same elites who considered the Serbs their enemy in the 1990s, now have an average citizen of the West for their enemy.

Although I've criticized Western imperialism in the book - in the sense that the Western powers often tricked natives to take away their land and that the Western powers generally violate treaty obligations. I'm not one of those people who think that the power of the West has resulted from colonialism. In that case, the richest and the most powerful countries would have been Spain and Portugal since they had the most colonies and some of them were very wealthy. The power of the West ensued from Western philosophy in terms of the discovery and application of the scientific method, the development of European universities as the centers of critical thought, the free market, and the mutual competition of

European countries. The special place takes the rise of the USA, which is a former colony itself. The philosophical concept of human rights implemented in the US Constitution, freedom of the market, faith in science and education as well as its favorable geographical position for self-defense in recent geopolitical contexts are the main reasons for the success of the USA. It's sad that in the 20th and 21st centuries in the United States, military interventionism has become the dominant way of conducting foreign policy. The world and ordinary US citizens are at a loss.

In conclusion, I have to say that although I've come up with a theory where there's causality between women's freedom and the weakening of civilization, I, by no means, believe that women's liberties should be abolished. The job of philosophy is to find and point out problems. That's what I have done. The solution to the problem must result from the knowledge of the existence of a problem, the scientific debate and the respect of the interests of men, women and children, who are often victims of male-female relationships. I'm not in favor of renewing some new patriarchy, but current feminism is doing more harm than good to women.

As for my moral theory, I wanted to help both philosophers and ordinary people understand better moral issues. Certainly, the claim that a lie itself isn't morally wrong is original. A lie is a tool, i.e. the weapon of the helpless. Only when used by the powerful, it becomes immoral. Moral responsibility rests on freedom. Person without freedom can't be morally responsible. That's why determinism obstructs morality. The one without power doesn't have significant freedom to decide and act, so it's pointless to overburden him with excessive moral guilt. That's why my morality - analogue morality - is completely analogous to the context of power.

LITERATURE

Note for cited literature: Since the first edition of the 2011 book is in Serbian, I mostly used the literature written in Serbian. However, since many books, which I've been using are published in English, I've decided to translate the titles into English (although the editions were mostly Serbian) so that the readers who are interested in it can understand which literature I've been using and eventually look for it in English. Although Wikipedia isn't always considered a reliable source of data and it isn't cited in serious works, I've used it as a source for the data I know by memory, when I didn't have the access to the original literature. It's also useful for checking dates, spelling and more.

Aristotle 1980: *Nicomachean Ethics*, Bigz, Belgrade

Crim, Keith 1992: Encyclopedia of Living Religions, Nolit, Belgrade

Djuric, Mihailo 2009: *Nietzsche and Metaphysics*, Official Gazette, Belgrade

Freud, Sigmund 1988: The Uneasiness in Civilization, Rad, Belgrade

Hegel, Georg Wilhelm Friedrich 2005: The Phenomenology of Spirit, Dereta, Belgrade

Hollingdale, Reginald John. 2004: Nietzsche: The Man and his Philosophy, Dereta, Belgrade

Honneth, Axel 2009: The Struggle for Recognition, Albatros plus, Belgrade

Jesic, Danko 2002: *Film and Comics*, Plato, Belgrade

Kant, Immanuel 1981: *Groundwork of the Metaphysics of Morals*, Bigz, Belgrade

Kant, Immanuel 2004: *Critique of Practical Reason*, Plato, Belgrade

Kant, Immanuel 1974: "On a supposed right to lie because of philanthropic concerns ", Mind and Freedom, special issue of Idea Magazine, Belgrade

Kant, Immanuel 1990: *The Critique of Pure Reason*, Bigz, Belgrade

Kojève, Alexandre, 1990: Introduction to the reading of Hegel, Veselin Maslesa, Sarajevo

Kostic, Zvonimir 1993: The 100 Most Prominent Serbs, Princip, Belgrade; S-Jupublik, Novi Sad

Liversage, Tony 2010: The Great Goddess, Archipelago, Belgrade (Den Store Gudinde: Copenhagen, Gyldendal, 1990)

Lukács, György 1956: Nietzsche and Nazism, Culture, Belgrade

MacIntyre, Alasdair 2000: A Short History of Ethics, Plato, Belgrade

Marx, Karl 1947: The Communist Manifesto, Kultura, Belgrade

Marx, Karl 1985: Early Writings, Napred, Zagreb

Mill, John Stewart 2003: Utilitarianism, Dereta, Belgrade

Milosevic, Nikola 2003: Literature and Metaphysics, Official Gazette of SCG, Belgrade

National Poet, 1987: Serbian Epic Ballads, Bigz, Belgrade

Nietzsche, Friedrich 2002: The Antichrist, Dereta, Belgrade

Nietzsche, Friedrich 1986: On the Genealogy of Morality, Grafos, Belgrade

Nietzsche, Friedrich 2002: A Book on the Philosopher, Dereta, Belgrade

Nietzsche, Friedrich 2007: Thus Spoke Zarathustra, Feniks-Libris, Novi Sad

Petronijevic, Branislav 1998: From Zeno to Bergson, Institute for Textbooks and Teaching Aids, Belgrade

Plato, the Republic

Ridley, Matt 2000: Genome, Plato, Belgrade

Ristic, Jovan; Vojnovic Marko 2002: Media Transformations of Conan the Barbarian "The Sign of the Sagite" no. 9, October, Belgrade

Tacitus, Cornelius 2007: The Germania, Chigoja Print, Belgrade

Toshevski, Jovo 2000: YOU ME, the National Book; Jefimija, Belgrade

Trebjeshanin, Zarko 2008: Glossary of Jungian Terms and Symbols HESPERIA edu, Belgrade

Tucic, Nikola 1987: An Introduction to Evolution Theory, Department of Textbooks and Teaching Aids, Belgrade